BLACK BELT
B·O·O·K·S

THE FIRST MIXED MARTIAL ART

PANKRATION FROM MYTHS TO MODERN TIMES

JIM ARVANITIS

BLACK BELT
B·O·O·K·S

THE FIRST MIXED MARTIAL ART

PANKRATION FROM MYTHS TO MODERN TIMES

JIM ARVANITIS

Edited by Jon Thibault and Jeannine Santiago

Photography by Rick Hustead

Graphic Design by John Bodine

Project Supervision: Raymond Horwitz

©2009 Black Belt Communications LLC
All Rights Reserved
Printed in South Korea
Library of Congress Control Number: 2009931569
ISBN-10: 0-89750-182-9
ISBN-13: 978-0-89750-182-8

First Printing 2009

BLACK BELT BOOKS

A Division of **OHARA PUBLICATIONS, INC.**

World Leader in Martial Arts Publications

CONTENTS

CONTENTS

ACKNOWLEDGMENTS

To my wonderful family and loyal followers.

To the Greek culture for inspiring me to carry the torch of our legacy, which, in turn, has given me passion for life.

Many thanks to the following:

The trainers and students of Spartan Academy USA who participated in the photos.

Christos Mavrofrides and Eric D. Hill, for their assistance in the translations.

Massad F. Ayoob and Nick Hines, for writing the forewords.

Rick Hustead and Chrystine M. Gardner, for shooting the photographs.

Bravo! Opa!

Demetrios "Jim" Arvanitis

ABOUT THE AUTHOR

Demitrios "Jim" Arvanitis is world recognized as Greek *pankration's* "Renaissance man." The Greek-American has made it his life's work to rebuild the remnants of the ancient combat sport from its ashes.

Among the elite pioneers of mixed martial arts, Arvanitis cross-trained in a number of different styles before it was an accepted practice. Opposing the theory that martial arts originated in Asia, Arvanitis began an odyssey to discover the combat roots of his ancestors before he was 20 years old. From the ancient pankration, he carefully analyzed the descriptions of Greece's early writers and the paintings and sculptures of its most influential artists. These sources became his "blueprint" in resurrecting pankration into a modern form. It was Arvanitis alone who would introduce it to mainstream martial arts as early as 1970 and popularize it throughout the world in the years that followed.

Arvanitis has received myriad awards and has been honored by numerous organizations. In 2001, he was nominated by his home state of New Hampshire as its "Athlete of the Century," and in 2006, he was given "Living Legend" status by his fellow grandmasters in the World Head of Family Sokeship Council. In addition to his contributions to the martial arts world, he is also a former boxing and wrestling champion, and a multiple world record holder for thumb push-ups.

Highly respected for his teaching prowess, Arvanitis opened the first pankration *palaistra* (school) in 1972 and has also conducted seminars in many parts of the world. His students include boxers, wrestlers, martial artists from various styles, professional bodyguards and stuntmen, law-enforcement personnel and military units.

Today, Arvanitis is legendary for his inspiring list of achievements and by beating the odds in restoring a legacy from antiquity. Through his athletic feats, books, videos, hundreds of TV appearances, magazine articles and radio interviews, Arvanitis has truly earned the title of "Father of Modern Pankration."

For more information, visit www.jimarvanitis.com.

FOREWORD I

I t's an honor to write the foreword for Jim Arvanitis' new book. I consider him one of the pioneers in modern martial arts.

We go back more than 30 years. The early 1970s was a heady time on the martial arts scene. Bruce Lee had become a cult figure and had triggered a craze for the arts that was sweeping the nation. *Dojo* seemed to spring up on every corner. Enough Korean national champions emerged to populate, well, Korea. It seemed that everyone who had ever taken a karate lesson while stationed with the military in Okinawa rented a storefront and declared it a dojo.

There was, in short, a lot of bull going on.

But it was also a period when some of the finest legitimate martial artists of our time, perhaps even of all time, emerged. Jim was one of them. I wrote for a number of martial arts magazines back then, including *Black Belt, Karate Illustrated* and *Official Karate*. I wrote the first story on Jim for *Black Belt*, and it became the November 1973 cover story.

A natural athlete from a family that produced such men—his brother Dan is a four-time New Hampshire Amateur Golf Association champion—Jim had a passion for the fighting arts. Intensely proud of his Greek heritage, Jim made *pankration* his life study. Owing to the diversity of pankration's skill set, he studied a broad variety of martial arts in-depth. And like Lee, he looked beyond the confines of tradition and what most accepted as the norm. Some accused his art of closely resembling Lee's, but it was actually quite the contrary. It was a case of great minds thinking alike.

Western wrestling combined with Greco-Roman (and some of the most effective Japanese grappling techniques, as well) made up much of the ground element of Jim's curriculum. His elbow, knee and kicking techniques came from the brutal sport of *muay Thai*, and his punches came from boxing—not flashy but strong. The emphasis was on penetrating power. From maximizing punching force by turning the hips to the little signature shuffles and hops he developed as he closed in with his kicks, Jim's subtle approach made the welterweight hit like a heavyweight by fighting smarter, not harder. He was a generation ahead of his time.

In scope, his approach ranged from the intellectual to the primitive. On one hand, he encouraged deep thinking and soul-searching to prepare his students for mortal combat, for facing death, and perhaps for having to end another human being's life. On the other hand, Jim taught biting techniques and destructive gouges that were more along the lines of his Spartan forebears—literally reverting to fang and claw if the combat threatened survival.

He had his fans and his critics. The latter, for the most part, had nothing worse to say than that he was arrogant. Jim was and is a proud man, but I wouldn't call him arrogant. "Arrogant" is a word often misused by insecure people to describe individuals with a level of self-confidence that they themselves cannot possibly relate to and will probably never achieve.

I found Jim always open to experimentation, to different approaches and to questions. In the 1970s, Jim and I lived in the greater Boston area. For a while, I was an assistant professor, teaching weapons and chemical agents in the Advanced Police Training Program at one of the colleges. I was concerned with empty-handed defense against a knife, because some of my students were corrections officers and jailers not routinely armed on duty with deadly weapons. In fact, they were often forbidden to carry even a baton. The majority of the students—career street cops who carried handguns and knew how to use them—understood that, at close range, a drawn knife is faster than a holstered gun and that an officer must be able to parry and survive the attack before he can draw and fire. I discussed this with Jim, and we agreed to put our heads together and spar to come up with a good technique. Each of us brought our knowledge (and our egos) to the mat.

Jim Arvanitis is one of the best martial artists I have ever seen. Until then, he had never met an opponent he couldn't disarm with one of his lightning-fast hand strikes or submission holds. However, he had not yet worked against someone who had really trained in the eclectic knife-fighting techniques that were emerging back then.

I considered myself pretty good with a blade. My father had taught me knife fighting from a very early age, and I was doing the research and training in it that would make it a subspecialty throughout my adult career. I had not yet sparred with a martial artist I couldn't "carve up" pretty good with a blunted training knife, or one who could disarm me.

But I had not yet pulled a blade on Jim Arvanitis.

Jim was not happy to discover that, half the time, he was unable to disarm me. And I was totally disenchanted to discover that, the other half of the time, he *could*.

This did not please either of us, and because the mutual goal was an effective unarmed defense sequence against a knife, we worked together intensely. What we came up with was the "double-A" defense (so called because both our surnames began with the letter), and I've been including it in training ever since. Jim tells me he still teaches it, too, so don't tell me this guy is arrogant. Jim Arvanitis listens, he looks and he absorbs. This is the kind of open-mindedness and forward thinking that has allowed his modernized pankration to become so effective.

Before most people had even heard the word "kinesiology," Jim was applying it. Back when people were asking, "Could *aikido* beat *wing chun*?" or "Would a Western boxer beat a *karateka*?" Jim was combining those arts and more. He is unquestionably one of the modern pioneers of mixed martial arts for both combat sports and self-defense, and he's been doing it for so long that he and his teaching team are far more experienced than most in how to blend those arts effectively.

Read Jim's book, absorb it and think about living by its principles. Don't fall into the trap of thinking "striking power is everything," "grappling skill is everything" or "ground fighting is everything." If my adult life of working in the use-of-force field has taught me anything, it has taught me this: *Everything is something. Nothing is everything.*

Jim was way ahead of most of his contemporaries in figuring that out, as you're about to see.

Massad F. Ayoob
Director, Lethal Force Institute

FOREWORD II

I met Jim Arvanitis in 1970. At the time, he wasn't in magazines but was reputed locally to be an extraordinary martial artist and a fierce street fighter. I was a black belt in *tang soo do*, a Korean karate style, and like many of my classmates, I practiced my skills in the *dojang* and in tournaments, while Jim proved himself elsewhere.

We all waited in anticipation for Jim, who was coming to demonstrate a style that, at the time, was Greek to all of us. The well-built athlete strolled in, and immediately we sensed his presence. Jim had confidence written all over him, and we knew right off that this was not one of the typical martial artists who visited the dojang. He introduced himself, explained what he was about to do and asked for volunteers to spar. Not one but *five* black belts lined up to take a shot at him. Jim insisted that his opponents attack as if it were an actual fight, and he made it clear that he would use full contact to defend himself. He put on these strange-looking gloves with fingers and nodded that he was ready. In a flash, it was over. While the Korean stylists assailed him with their trademark kicks, he nailed them with fast hand combinations, elbows and knees, and cut their legs from under them, sending them flying. Jim saved the best for last; he jammed a kick and performed a leg takedown, took his foe's back and choked him out on the ground. We were all in a state of shock. These were black belts, and he defeated them with ease.

After the demonstration, we asked about his style, and Jim told us it was not a style but a composite of fighting skills. He called it *pankration*. Some of us asked to become his pupils, but he declined. About two years later, however, he finally consented to teach a small group of us; little did I know, I was witnessing history in the making.

Learning under Jim was a radical departure from my previous training. Everything was geared toward free fighting, with a heavy emphasis on conditioning and no forms. We used full contact at all times, and he drilled us on combat concepts like timing, leverage, momentum and the importance of strategy. There was an equal balance of standing and ground tactics, and of striking and grappling. Jim introduced more and more Greek terminology as time passed, which made us aware that this was not an eclectic amalgam of techniques but an art deeply rooted in his lineage. I think Jim's street-fighting background inspired him to search for the ultimate combat method—what he liked to call the "martial truth." He could have named it anything and become famous, but he paid homage to his culture by using their ancient term. This, he said, brought credibility to the ancients for their historic achievement.

Jim has always been a warrior and at his best in a fight. He has never backed down from anyone, and I've seen him in action many times over the years. As his notoriety grew, he frequently answered challenges. I'll never forget one fight that occurred when a muscular bodybuilder and his "posse" walked into our *palaistra* (training hall), looking for trouble. The man boasted that he made his living as a bouncer at the Zoo—a seedy nightclub in one of the toughest areas of Boston—and claimed to be an expert in Mongolian wrestling and many karate styles. The scars covering his torso attested to his many scraps. When he proposed that the two of them go at it, no holds barred, Jim promptly accepted.

After dismissing the class, Jim asked three of us to remain for backup. Our guests showed their disdain, probably thinking it was going to be an easy win for their fighter. Jim's opponent dwarfed him in size, but the Spartan-Greek looked like a tiger ready to pounce. He glanced over at me and winked, as if he knew he was about to impart a beating. They measured off, and after a few probing attacks, Jim's rival charged. The next thing I knew, the bouncer was down and Jim was on top of him, landing a vicious barrage of fists, elbows and knees. The fight lasted less than 30 seconds.

We all wondered what had put the challenger on his back. Like Muhammad Ali's famous "phantom punch," most of us failed to see Jim's backhand finger flick strike the attacker square in the eyeball, dropping him. After regaining consciousness, the bouncer remarked that he had never in his life felt such pain. It paralyzed him, and he couldn't protect himself.

Jim is one of a kind—a truly unique individual. He is a visionary who never lost sight of the fact that pankration would live again. What you are about to read is the story of a legacy that flourished early in human history, vanished and was reborn through the inspiring efforts of one special man. I consider myself privileged to be a small part of this saga.

Arhegos Master Nick Hines
Paidotribes, United Pankration Alliance

INTRODUCTION

Excitement filled the air of the stadium. It was the Olympiad of 564 B.C., and Philostratos, a noted fight reporter, anticipated a one-sided contest in the climactic sports event of this historic day. The match would pit Arrichion of Phigaleia, the champion and resounding favorite, against a challenger whose name has been lost in time. Neither competitor realized the impact their performance would have in the annals of ancient Greek athletics.

The fighters entered the arena prepared to do battle, their naked bodies heavily oiled in the traditional manner and their beads of sweat glistening in the afternoon sun. The rules were quite simple: no biting or gouging, no time limit, and a competitor could win the match either by knockout or submission. Anything else was fair game, but the participants were warned by the *hellanodikes* (referee), who was capably armed with a stout rod for striking violators, that he would strictly enforce any infraction of the rules.

The contest commenced, and the two men circled one another cautiously, each looking for an opening to launch his potentially lethal assault. As the cheers from the crowd heightened, Arrichion took the offensive and delivered a thunderous kick to his opponent's leg, expecting his rival to fall to the ground where he could finish him off. The challenger, however, maintained his footing and limped off to a safer, more strategic position. After another exchange of blows with fists and feet that clearly favored the champion, Arrichion, sensing a quick triumph, closed in for the kill.

Now in grappling range, the combatants clinched. Arrichion attempted to tackle his foe by the legs, but the challenger, seemingly out of nowhere, spun Arrichion around and sprang on his back. Arrichion felt himself being choked from behind as the challenger clamped his forearm over the champion's throat. Arrichion knew at once he had fallen prey to the dreaded *klimakismos* (ladder grip) as his opponent scissored his legs around the champion's waist, locking his insteps behind Arrichion's thighs as he strangled the life from him.

In a desperate effort to free himself, Arrichion gripped the challenger's foot behind his right leg, locked his knee around his opponent's ankle and then threw himself backward. In viselike fashion, he clasped his legs together and kicked back with his right foot, twisting the opposing fighter's ankle. When they both landed, the ankle was broken in the champion's hand.

It would be Arrichion's final act. As the two athletes hit the ground, Arrichion succumbed to the choke hold and died, while his opponent, screaming in agony, raised his hand in defeat. The judges were faced with the arduous task of deciding who, in fact, had won the bout. Did Arrichion expire before his foe had submitted? After a brief conference, the victory was awarded to the corpse of Arrichion.

So it was written by Philostratos.

Such dramatic accounts of legendary *pankration* events rival the mythology of the gods. Pronounced *pan-gra-tee-on* in the old dialect and *pan-cray-shun* in its modern Anglicized derivative, pankration is an ancient Hellenic (Greek) combat sport that dates back 3,000 years. The term itself is an archaic Greek word that means "all powers" or "total strength." Pankration stands out as the most recognized of the Greek martial arts and the first recorded form of mixed fighting, combining striking and submission-grappling techniques. It was developed as the ultimate test of athletic skill and endurance to fill the void left by the boxing and wrestling contests. It was also the cornerstone of the earliest Olympic Games.

To this day, there continues to be much debate over pankration's origin. Some contend that it can be traced to the 12th millennium B.C., when pankration was referenced in Apollonius' poem *Argonautica*, but most historians and scholars agree that pankration does not appear in Homer's writings or other literature before the fifth century. There is, however, another contingent of "die-hard Greeks" who think otherwise; they remain steadfast that their sport of antiquity goes back even further in time and is steeped in mythology and legend.

The Greeks were among the first people to create myths as a means to explain the inexplicable and to interpret the phenomena of life. These myths were passed from one generation to the next and altered according to the needs and developments of each moment in time. The Hellenic mentality produced supreme beings—gods who controlled the universe and human destiny. The gods were worshipped, their feats serving to inspire the Greeks to conquer barriers in attaining their incredible goals. For them, mythology stimulated their restless minds, resulting in the making of the influential Hellenic culture. Likewise, they believed that all the competitive sports events of antiquity were founded or invented by a god or some heroic figure.

This book is based on this premise. It examines the evolution of ancient Greek combat, from its mythical beginnings to its stature in athletics, from its importance to the Greek soldier on the blood-soaked battlefield to its deterioration during the Roman era and revival in the 20th century. Although pankration is the primary focus of this work, other forms of early Greco-Roman martial systems and practices, including war dances and weaponry, are presented. Each is an important branch of past and present Hellenic combatives.

Also essential to the study of Greek combat in antiquity is the role it played in the Olympic Games as well as in other Panhellenic festivals. This text includes much historical material on these monumental competitions, because it was there that the "heavy" events of boxing, wrestling and pankration came to prominence in the Hellenistic world. To this day, the Olympics stand as the glory of Greece.

The content of this book is arranged in two main sections. The first details the myths and traditions that were so influential on the early development of the sport. Greek-related topics such as *areti* (the competitive ideal) and the four major Panhellenic festivals are discussed extensively throughout these chapters. The second section covers the evolution of Hellenic combat arts and sports, and it discusses the techniques, training and various methodologies used in both the contest arena and in battle. *Pyrrichios*, *hoplomachia* and the lethal *pammachon* (on which sport pankration is based) are featured, as are rarely revealed accounts of ancient battles derived from sources such as Homer, Pausanias and other Greek poets and writers of the period.

Additional chapters discuss the demise of Hellenic combat sport during the rule of the powerful but sadistic Roman Empire until the revival of the Olympic Games in 1896 and the restoration of pankration as a modern fighting art and "reality-based" contest in the late 1960s. A random sampling of applied modern pankration skills and techniques are also included. An important supplement to the information presented is the appendix. It includes a very detailed timeline, a chronological listing of Olympic combat victors in antiquity and a glossary of Greek terminology used by ancient and present trainers.

At this point, let me make it clear that this is not merely a book of techniques, fighting applications or training methods. Although much of this information is covered, it is not intended as the main focus of this work. This material is geared more toward the combat aficionado whose interest is in the traditions and contributions of possibly the most influential culture of early Western civilization.

Since the late 1960s, when I first regenerated what my ancestors had devised thousands of years before, the number of practitioners of pankration—whether at a legitimate school or one that conveniently adopted the term—has grown from perhaps only myself to several thousands internationally. Web sites are on the rise, and organizations are springing up seemingly everywhere.

When Athens, Greece, was named to host the 2004 Olympics, a movement emerged to re-enter pankration as a new sport. During this time, various bogus groups surfaced and many individuals claimed to be "carrying the torch" of Olympic pankration. None of these individuals, however, had the right to make such outlandish statements, and none of the groups even existed in the 1960s, '70s or '80s. Even in Greece, the motherland, the term "pankration" was not restored until the late 1990s. Pankration had become all the rage, especially with its connection to the Olympic name.

Though the Olympic movement faltered, interest in sport pankration continues its global growth. Currently, organizations exist in many countries, including Greece, the United States, Canada, Spain, Italy, Brazil, Mexico, Portugal, Russia, Lithuania, Iran, Pakistan, France and Japan.

With the original pankration defunct, what is this animal known as modern pankration? Is it a system, a sport or an eclectic blend of techniques? For most, it appears to be an almost limitless unarmed-fighting hybrid with an equal emphasis on standing and ground skills. On the surface, it is very much like today's mixed martial arts, having both sport and combat applications. However, modern pankration is much more than this. As the nucleus of Greek martial arts, it preserves a history rich in fact and myth, stemming from its battlefield version to its early Olympian days and extending to the present.

It must also be understood that the original pankration became a lost art for many decades, perhaps even centuries. Little is documented about it between the time that the Panhellenic games were discontinued and the second half of the 19th century. By no means does this imply that the tradition of these arts was gone forever. During the 12th century and after the Byzantine era, pankration experienced a revival and became known as *clotsata* (to cry out).

It later spread to Western Europe, where it was known as *lactes* during the Middle Ages and *patso clotso* during the early 19th century. We have only poetic verses and accounts by early scholars and the numerous vase paintings, coins and frescoes that suggest the techniques of antiquity. For this reason alone, there are many interpretations of what pankration is today. To some, it is just a convenient label for combining techniques for sport fighting, while others have developed it into a karate system complete with preset forms based on what they think is depicted in artistic renderings.

Greco-Roman combat sports were popular and thriving activities for almost 12 centuries. It is fair to say that they went hand in hand with religion and spirituality, much like martial arts did in medieval China and Japan. Thanks to the survival of various forms of ancient evidence, a fairly accurate reconstruction of the development and staging of such events has been possible. Archaeological studies of the remains of ancient stadiums, arenas, gymnasiums and the like are a vital source of information. Also, the large Greek national festivals, including the one held in Olympia, maintained detailed records of winners, events and dates.

Fighting scenes painted on pottery or carved into stone constitute still another source, as do various examples of ancient literature. These modes of expression, especially poetry written about contests and athletes, constituted in a sense the popular sports media of their time. Among the most influential Greek writers after Homer were the brilliant poet Pindar (fifth century B.C.), who wrote odes honoring Olympic winners; the second-century traveler and geographer Pausanias, who penned the world's first known guidebook; and the second-century physician Galen, whose works provided valuable data about the training, diet and injuries of combat athletes and gladiators.

Pankration is frequently described as "combat wrestling that allows strikes." There are accounts in the classical epics suggesting that pankration was more of an upright style that emphasized kicking, punching and throws. The fact is that sport pankration, also referred to as pankration *athlima*, is made up of two distinct elements. The first, called *ano* or *orthostadin* pankration, is primarily the stand-up component that is similar to kickboxing, but with the additional offensive skills of clinching, takedowns, throws and submission holds.

Kato pankration, the other component, is predominantly a ground game with armbars, leg locks, strangulation techniques and striking. Since its development several thousand years ago, the kato contest represented the ultimate method of submission fighting. There was also a form of hard-core battlefield pankration called *panmachia* or *pammachon*. This was essentially a total method of brutal unarmed combat, used exclusively by Greece's highly trained soldiers. Another objective of this book is to examine each of these significant aspects of this comprehensive system.

Certainly, modern pankration is not a precise duplication of the original. At best, it is a close simulation of those combative concepts that remain from its ruins. Not only is competing naked unacceptable in today's society but so is the lack of rules that governed a classic contest. The *true* art is not merely a collection of techniques for competition but involves a deep understanding of the traditions of an ancient culture in which roots of this practice were initially formulated. The impact of pankration techniques has been felt around the world, having spawned Western boxing and wrestling, in addition to many of the Asian martial arts. Be it a front kick, hammerfist or shoulder throw, the lineage of each can be traced back to the ancient Greeks.

This book presents the historical evolution of pankration to the reader, and it provided an almost endless process of learning for this author. I set out on my personal journey more than 35 years ago and have been compiling information to this day. I have attempted to include as much pertinent data between these pages as I was able to accumulate. Much of this is based on fact, while some is left to conjecture. No one can fully understand an ancient technique through vase paintings or archaic descriptions alone. We form our own interpretations and build on them. Being of Greek blood and a lifelong student of the martial arts, I remain as passionate as ever, and I am well aware that there is always more knowledge waiting to be discovered.

It is also a fact, whether today's competitors realize it or not, that contemporary mixed styles and limited-rules events owe their humble beginnings to this oldest of fighting disciplines. The material that follows is only a guide in the odyssey of pankration. Whether the inspiration of the gods or the invention of mere mortals, the combat arts and sports of antiquity stand today as they did several thousand years ago: another of ancient Greece's magnificent contributions to the world.

Dinami kai Areti (Strength and Honor),
Demetrios "Jim" Arvanitis

PART I
MYTHOLOGY AND TRADITIONS

1. THE GODS OF OLYMPUS

To the classical Greek mind, the gods represented nature, and each god or goddess was associated with one or more of its forces. The role of the gods was to maintain harmony and order, not in the world's definitive creation. Each had assigned properties with a profound symbolic meaning: They were the interpretation of unexplained natural phenomena and the guardians of the fragile balance between man and nature.

The gods were held in the highest esteem by the Greeks, who considered them immortal, supreme and magnificent. They could control all humanity in each detail of life, determining fortunes, relationships, and when people entered and departed the world. The gods represented the incarnation of human perfection, and the ancient Greeks bestowed to them all the properties they aspired to but were prevented from possessing by their own human weaknesses and limitations.

Although they were divine beings, the gods appeared physically similar to man. They were idealistic shapes in the ancient Greek mind but assumed human form when they found it necessary to appear to mortals. Their bodies were not tangible or corporeal but were energy fields that emitted supernatural powers, much like God is viewed today in many religions.

Among all the gods worshipped by the Greeks, the 12 who dwelled on Mount Olympus—the highest mountain in Hellas—were in a class by themselves. There were six men and six women, and they were divided into six couples united by bonds of friendship or kinship: Zeus and Hera, Poseidon and Demeter, Apollo and Artemis, Hermes and Athena, Ares and Aphrodite, and Hephaestus and Hestia.

The gods of Olympus lived primarily in peace in a place that bordered earth and sky and from where they could oversee all that took place in the world below. Their main interest was in man, whom they sometimes showered with gifts and sometimes persecuted.

The leader of the gods was Zeus, the omnipotent. The spiritual father of gods and men alike, Zeus dispensed divine justice throughout the universe. Unlike many of the classical Greek gods, he was truly Greek in origin. His name is also related to the Greek word *dios*, meaning "bright." Throughout antiquity, Zeus was worshipped as a weather god who had the power to produce heavenly light and to regulate the wind, clouds, rain, thunder and lightning. His symbols were the thunderbolt, which represented the forces of weather, and the eagle, the sacred bird that soared higher in the sky than any other and faster than all but lightning. He is portrayed in Homer's epic poem, the *Iliad* (circa 750 B.C.), as sending thunderstorms against his enemies, and he is often shown in artwork hurling his thunderbolt.

Zeus was the son of Rhea and Cronus, the cruel Titan who devoured his newborn offspring out of fear that one might overtake his throne. Zeus luckily escaped this fate because his mother had hid him in a cave in Crete while Cronus was given a stone wrapped in swaddling clothes to eat in his place. Years later, Zeus defeated Cronus in battle and proceeded to gain victory over the Titans, a race of primeval gods who preceded the Olympian gods. Zeus then overcame the terrible giants, a race of huge monsters with snakes for hair and dragonlike tails. With the help of other gods, he conquered Typhon, the son of Tartarus and Ge, who sought to destroy the world. After these victories, Zeus became world ruler.

The *Gigantomachia* (battle with the giants) was one of the most popular stories in Greek

The mighty Zeus, father of the gods, holding a scepter and thunderbolt.

art and poetry, symbolizing the victory of civilization over savagery. On the architectural sculptures on the Parthenon, the battle might be shown in conjunction with the fight between centaurs and Lapiths or the conflict between Greeks and Amazons. Zeus' moral dimension as orderer of the universe made him most important to Greek civilization. During the Mycenaean Age (a subdivision of the Bronze Age that spanned from 1600 B.C. to 1100 B.C.), Zeus reigned as the supreme king over a human society organized around kings. He ruled the subordinate gods and oversaw human events in the world below from his cloud-shrouded palace on Mount Olympus.

As the age of Greek kings diminished between 1100 B.C. and 900 B.C., Zeus retained his pre-eminence and developed into a chief judge, peacemaker and civic god. Myths describe how he destroyed primeval monsters and forged peace in place of violence. He maintained the laws, instituted festivals, provided prophecies and generally oversaw the fruits of civilized life. Circa 200 B.C., the Stoic philosophers of Greece regarded Zeus as the single, universal deity.

Together with his power over heaven and earth, Zeus was the protector of human dwellings. He also was responsible for administering justice if human oaths were not followed. Although his punishments could be harsh in the extreme, he was always willing to forgive if mortals displayed their remorse and prayed to him. For all these reasons, the Greeks constantly paid homage to the leader of the gods by honoring him through festivals and sporting events. Two of the four major Panhellenic festivals were dedicated to Zeus, namely the Olympics and the Nemean games. It was chiefly through these spectacles that Greek combat sport would make its impact on early athletic competition.

2. ARETI AND THE COMPETITIVE SPIRIT

Ancient Greece stands out as an agonistic culture, one which distinguished itself above others for its love of competition and through the nature of its contests. The poems of Homer make it clear that the competitive spirit became highly developed within the framework of Greek mythology. It captivated the minds and hearts of the men of the period, and they projected their own longing to compete in the name of their deities and heroes.

The myths describe the gods fighting among themselves in an effort to support mortals in their own conflicts as well as competing for the right to become lord and protector of a city or country. One of the most famous disputes of this ilk occurred when Poseidon and Athena vied for patronage of the city of Athens. They desired to realize the ideal formulated by Hippolochos—to "always be the best and excel over others." The mythical heroes expressed this same trait in all their actions, from group expeditions, like those of the Argonauts, to personal feats to benefit man, like those of Herakles and Theseus.

The gods' spousal selection and succession to the throne were decided by mythical sporting contests. Atalanta had declared she would marry anyone who could defeat her in a foot race. She competed against and defeated all of her suitors until she was beaten by Hippomenes, who made her his wife. Likewise, Ikarios gave Penelope to Odysseus only after he had outrun her other suitors, and Pelops married Oinomaos' daughter Hippodameia following his victory in the chariot race. The Skythian hero Skythes, son of Herakles and Echidna, ascended to the throne after defeating his two brothers in archery, according to the dictates of his father.

Being "the first" was another characteristic of the competitive spirit. Gods and heroes are depicted in mythology as being the "first inventors" of varying features of both materialistic and spiritual culture. In the Classical period, almost every contest was theorized to have had a god or hero creator, one who had discovered it and given it to mankind. It was believed that Apollo had invented boxing, for instance.

For the Greeks, education entailed the cultivation of one's total being and could not be divided into physical and mental learning. Socrates, perhaps the most dominant intellectual figure in the old world, remarked, "The mind cannot exist without the body and, likewise, the body is meaningless without the mind." It was in the gymnasia of Athens while admiring the athletes' physical beauty and strength that Socrates drew his inspiration to train their minds.

The ancient Greeks traced their athletic origins back to mythical times and to the gods themselves, from whom the most important heroic figures descended. It was only natural, then, that they associated the very roots of combat sport with the ancient legends and that they attributed them to the gods and heroes themselves. Competing, therefore, had a spiritual value for the Greeks, and it brought man in contact with the gods, which explains why the contests were always held in the most sacred sanctuaries: Olympia, Delphi, Nemea and the Isthmus.

The competitive ideal, one of the most significant factors in Hellenic history, embraced both a spiritual and religious depth that elevated it far above the level of the simple game that was played. Man himself was the visible image of the gods, for the gods possessed all of a mortal's characteristics, but in an idealistic form. Physical perfection for the Greeks meant a proximity to the gods, and physical strength was an expression of that proximity.

Following the time of Homer, athletic competitions became increasingly popular throughout the Greek world. With this emerged a new, uniquely Hellenic concept called *kalokagathia*. Derived from the words *kalos*, meaning "beautiful," and *agathos*, meaning "noble" or "learned," the concept translates roughly as the "mind-body ideal." At first fashionable mainly in aristocratic circles but later popular with Greeks of other classes, kalokagathia emphasized striving for a combination of physical and mental excellence to develop a rounded and complete personality. Many Greeks therefore came to glorify a keen mind in a strong, athletic body.

Connected to this spirit of competition was another Greek word: *areti*. While its precise meaning cannot be translated within the scope of the contemporary English language, the term refers to the attributes of excellence, prowess, pride, virtue, nobility and honor. Homer applied this term exclusively to the effectiveness and qualities of a trained warrior: physical strength, skill in the use of weaponry and heroism in battle. Although areti existed to some degree in all ancient Greeks, it was the athlete who aspired to its highest level of development. Some even believed that the gods had blessed selected mortals with this gift, making them demigods. Areti represented the soul of the classic competitor and his individual quest for perfection and purity of both mind and body.

It was precisely this heroic aspiration that became the focus of all athletic contests. The extraordinary, almost superhuman attempt to accomplish a goal or establish a feat by superb physical and mental effort is the dominant theme in Greek mythology. This way of thinking raised the level of human competition into the realm of the gods and provided them with an ideal that was handed down from one generation to the next throughout the athletic heyday of the Classical period and beyond. Indeed, for close to a century, Greece was first and foremost an agonistic civilization—one that, more than any other culture, was dedicated to competition.

In the *Iliad*, a famous exhortation is made by Peleus to his son Achilles, who sets off to do battle in the Trojan War: "Always to be best and excel over others." Such a statement summarizes the attitude and ideals of the Greeks throughout the course of antiquity. This competitive spirit extended to every aspect of Greek life. Greece valued superiority of mind and body and encouraged all its citizens to display their innate talents. Athletes participated in the Panhellenic games without discrimination, other than the requirement to be a free Greek citizen. Musicians and poets, painters and sculptors, contended for this same excellence by assembling in the great centers of Hellenism, where they achieved fame and honor in intellectual and artistic circles.

Along with physical characteristics, psychological traits were also deemed relevant, especially by Homer—in the cunning of Odysseus and the wisdom of Nestor, for example. Such qualities were not included in the idea of areti but were highly prized within the ranks of the Greek aristocracy. During the seventh and sixth centuries B.C., profound changes took place in the social structure of the Greek city-states. The aristocrats lost their privileged position and almost limitless political powers, causing them to adopt a new lifestyle. Physical culture became a tradition and one of the outward signs of social status.

Many of the aristocrats spent much of their free time in exclusive clubs called *hetairai*, where they discussed the meaning of life and human society in general. Among them emerged a group of poets—Archilochus, Alcaeus, Sappho, Simonides, Xenophanes and others—whose poetry brought a new dimension to the old aristocratic ideal of areti. In addition to physical prowess, the term now incorporated refined social behavior, as well—the art of conversation, recitation, song, dance and the playing of musical instruments.

Greek philosophers also contributed to the further development of areti. Through their studies of man and the evolution of society, they increasingly emphasized the importance of moral and spiritual factors, such as justice, generosity, nobility of mind and learning. The foundation of both Socratic and Platonic philosophy was based on the belief that the highest human potential was achieved through knowledge and that all other human abilities were derived from this central capacity. Aristotle also supported this belief and stated that the highest human potential was located in theoretical knowledge. The new concept of areti became the foundation of the education of the aristocratic youth and in Athenian democracy.

In Greece's Classical Age (500 B.C. to 300 B.C.), athletic training and sports contests became common facets of everyday life—and the gymnasium, where patrons received academic and physical training, became an obligatory institution in every Greek city-state.

3. THE ROOTS OF UNARMED FIGHTING

To the Greeks, all sports were the creation of some god or mythical figure. According to Pausanias, Herakles (known as Hercules in Roman mythology) invented the unarmed combat form that would later become *pankration*, while the biographer and essayist Plutarch (A.D. 50 to 125) claimed that the legendary hero Theseus created it. Both characters are part of Greek folklore and stories abound of their incredible feats.

HERAKLES

The most popular of all Greek mythical heroes, Herakles (meaning "glory of Hera") was famous for his strength, courage and generosity. Herakles was the son of Zeus and a mortal woman named Alkmene, and his statue was a common presence in the gymnasiums of classical Greece.

The goddess Hera was Herakles' enemy from the outset. She continued to be his nemesis throughout his life and reconciled with him only after his death and transformation into a god. It was she who blighted him with madness, forcing him to kill his wife Megara and their children. Seeking atonement, he went to the sanctuary at Delphi and was ordered by Apollo to serve for 12 years under King Eurytheus. The king set upon Herakles a series of tasks, which he was to complete in 12 years.

By virtue of his Twelve Labors, each of which involved destroying something horrid or retrieving a prize, Herakles was worshipped as both god and man throughout antiquity. The Labors started with the elimination of certain monsters throughout the Peloponnese, but the goals gradually became more symbolic. Herakles, assisted in some cases by the goddess Athena, accomplished the tasks successfully and won purification for his crime. Many of these exploits document the use of unarmed combat skills.

The first task required Herakles to kill and skin the terrible lion of Nemea. Legend suggests that it was this feat that established him as a founder of the fighting form that would later become pankration. The beast, bred by Hera, was in the habit of devouring local people and animals, and it lived in a cave with only two entrances. No weapon could pierce its hide, and no club could crush its skull. Herakles' attacks had no effect, so he decided that the only way to kill the beast was to move in close, risking its teeth and claws, and wrestle it to death.

He blocked one of the mouths to the cave, entered by the other and proceeded to seize the beast by the throat and strangle it. Paintings on vases depict various grappling techniques used in the struggle. Scenes reveal Herakles executing a shoulder throw on the beast, a standing head lock, and his fingers interlocked in the common wrestler's grip. He skinned the dead lion and wore its hide over his shoulders and its head as a helmet. Throughout his life, the Greek hero was never seen without his lion skin. Zeus commemorated this first labor of Herakles by immortalizing the lion in the sky as the constellation Leo.

Besides the Twelve Labors, Herakles had many mythical exploits, partly because so many cities of Greece wanted to claim an association with him. His defeat of the evil wrestler Antaios, the giant son of Poseidon, was another tale of his extraordinary combative prowess. According to the poet Pindar, Antaios forced guests who had the misfortune of visiting his domain to wrestle with him. He then killed them and buried their bodies in his training hall.

His club lying nearby on the ground, Herakles grapples with the dreaded Nemean lion.

Later accounts of this story depicted Antaios as the son of Earth. Because he could continually draw sustenance from his mother, he proved more than a match for Herakles.

When Herakles threw Antaios to the ground, he gained renewed strength with each fall. Any other opponent would have easily suffered broken bones, but the giant repeatedly lumbered back to his feet and attacked Herakles. Herakles was in disbelief that he was in danger of being beaten by a mere giant because he had just sent some of the immortal gods scurrying back to Olympus, defeated. Paintings show the much-smaller Herakles resorting to some questionable tactics against the barbarian ogre, namely gouging at his eyes while holding his beard. In the end, however, Hellenic skill would overcome magic as Herakles defeated and killed his adversary by lifting him completely off the ground. As Antaios weakened, Herakles easily broke his neck and killed him.

Herakles also found himself in more than one encounter involving death and the underworld. When Eryx, a famous boxer and son of Aphrodite, challenged Herakles to fight, they wagered that, if Eryx lost, his land would be forfeited, and if Herakles lost, he would donate his cattle and his immortality. Herakles was triumphant, and he also won in battles against Hades, the god of the underworld, and against Menoites, the herdsman of the underworld.

Although neither man nor beast seemed capable of defeating the mighty Herakles in combat, he was forced to succumb to impossible odds. In one wrestling event at Olympia, Herakles was unsuccessful in his bid to compete against two opponents at the same time. After his loss, a proverb was handed down that sums up the Greeks' own experiences through their seemingly unbeatable hero: "Not even Herakles can take on two."

When the centaur Nessos attempted to ravish Herakles' second wife, Deianira, the hero killed him with arrows dipped in the venom of the Lernean Hydra, which he had killed to fulfill his

The mythological wrestling contest between Herakles and Antaios.

second labor. But the dying centaur tricked Deianira into taking some of his blood, convincing her that it could be used as a love potion on Herakles, if necessary. Later, seeking to retain the affections of her unfaithful husband, she saturated with the blood a tunic that Herakles customarily wore when offering ceremonial thanks to Zeus. As soon as he put it on, he began to suffer excruciating pain from the venom. He tried to remove the tunic but only succeeded in ripping away chunks of his own flesh. Realizing his end was near, Herakles climbed to the summit of Mount Oete and commanded that he be set on fire. On the funeral pyre, the mortal remains of Herakles were burned away and he ascended as a god to Mount Olympus.

Herakles served as the ultimate example of the Greek honor code of areti. Warrior soldiers not only mimicked his physical appearance but also strived to follow his example in their daily lives. In addition to having influenced the development of sport pankration, Herakles was credited for founding the original Olympic Games.

Athens National Archaeological Museum

Herakles, locked in combat with the centaur Nessos.

THESEUS OF ATTICA

Theseus (meaning "settler"), perhaps the greatest king of Athens, is also considered by many Greeks to be the founder of ancient pankration. The son of Poseidon and Aethra, he was viewed as an Athenian national hero and a warrior who rid the countryside of brigands and unified the villages of Attica into a single federation. The Theseus legend was reworked many times by generations of poets and storytellers who seemingly modeled many of his exploits after those of Herakles, in an attempt to equate the popularity and relevance of the two.

Theseus was born in Troezen and grew up both strong and courageous. While visiting Delphi, the adolescent Theseus lifted a rock to reveal the sword and sandals of his mortal father, Aegeus, an Attican prince. (In Greek lore, it is not uncommon for a hero to have two fathers, one mortal and one immortal.) Theseus soon departed for Athens to lay claim to his royal inheritance. On his journey, he disposed of criminals who had been ambushing unsuspecting travelers. The first of these to feel the wrath of Theseus was Periphetes, who killed passers-by with a huge brass club. Theseus grappled with and killed Periphetes, and he took possession of the club, which served him well in his continued adventures.

Another well-documented victory (similar to Herakles' defeat of Antaios) is Theseus' win over Kerykon, who challenged travelers to wrestle him in his *palaistra* and killed them in the process. This dangerous adversary had his own personal submission style and, based on Greek belief, developed the strategy of attacking the legs. Utilizing his superior skill, Theseus defeated Kerykon by lifting him high into the air and smashing him headfirst into the ground.

When the triumphant Theseus arrived in Athens, his father Aegeus was already king, and Theseus became a marked man by his cousins, the Pallantids, who feared he would overtake

Metropolitan Museum of Art, New York

Theseus throws an opponent to the ground in a pankration contest.

Museo Archeologico Nazionale di Napoli, Naples, Italy

A Roman mosaic depicting Theseus as he grapples with the Minotaur and scissors one of its legs.

the throne. They plotted to kill him, but Theseus launched his own surprise attack and slew them all. After being brought to trial and acquitted, Theseus captured the dangerous Cretan bull and sacrificed it to Apollo in an Athenian temple.

Theseus was not the only one who had tried to kill the Cretan bull. Androgeos, the son of King Minos of Crete, had made an earlier attempt but was gored and killed by the bull in the process. King Minos, blinded by anger and pain, imposed a harsh punishment on the citizens of Athens: He forced them to sacrifice seven young men and seven young women every year to the dreaded Minotaur—the monstrous half-man, half-bull. The young Athenians were imprisoned in an inescapable Labyrinth that housed the Minotaur, and they were eaten by the beast. Theseus pledged to put a stop to this oppression and proceeded to sail to Crete among the latest batch of young sacrifices.

Once in Crete, Theseus met the daughter of King Minos and Queen Pasiphae, Princess Ariadne. The princess fell in love with Theseus and gave him a ball of thread to guide him through the dark Labyrinth corridors. He fastened one end of the thread to the entrance and ventured inside, where he eventually found the ferocious Minotaur and slew it after a fierce and bloody battle. Because the struggle involved a variety of techniques—punches, kicks and wrestling—many credit Theseus as pankration's creator. There is disagreement, however, on whether the Minotaur was killed by Theseus' bare hands or with his dagger. One description tells of Theseus throwing the beast to the ground and twisting its head by the horns until its neck was broken. There is also a vase painting that shows blood pouring from the dying Minotaur's throat, where what appears to be a blade had found its mark.

In any case, Theseus has always occupied a special place in the hearts of Athenians, who regard him as their greatest hero and patron. He also gained recognition as the founder of the Isthmian games in honor of his father, Poseidon. The spirit of Theseus is said to have appeared in full battle dress before Athenian warriors at the Battle of Marathon in 490 B.C. The warriors were then empowered to drive the Persians back, slaying thousands of their invaders while sustaining minimal losses.

Louvre Museum, Paris

A plate depicting Theseus as he defeats the terrible Minotaur with a dagger.

British Museum, London

This cylix chronicles the feats of Theseus, with the killing of the Minotaur in the center. Clockwise from top: Theseus grappling with Kerkyon, preparing to strike Procrustes with an ax, threatening Sciron with a basin (while the sea monster lies in wait behind a rock for its prey), capturing the bull of Marathon, bending a tree to which Sines is tied, and attacking the sow Phaea.

4. EARLY COMBAT CONTESTS

T he precise origin of athletic competition in Greece is lost in time. Certainly, organized contests and other sports existed long before the Panhellenic games. The gathering of athletes from all over the Greek world in the earliest Olympiads suggests that a long tradition of such events existed. In fact, the beginnings can be traced to the Minoan and Mycenaean

Athens National Archaeological Museum

Two young Aegean fighters wearing girdles and gloves.

On this rhyton from Hagia Triada, the bottom two bands show combatants during the Minoan period. On the third band down, the boxer on the left has knocked his opponent to the ground. His left arm is slightly bent to protect himself, while his right arm is preparing to deliver a blow. The lowest band illustrates two scenes: On the left, the defeated youth on the ground is attempting to defend against further strikes; on the right, it appears that the standing fighter has turned his foe upside down with a waist lock. This sport appeared to have been a combination of striking and grappling, similar to the later pankration.

periods (about 2600 B.C. to 1100 B.C.) in the Aegean Islands and in distant Crete. Both cultures were influenced by the games of Egypt and by the people of the East. Wall paintings depict men wrestling, lifting weights and performing other exercises. One finds in Crete the first indications of the athletic spirit that evolved and reached its highest point in subsequent centuries. These games developed into more exacting performances with established rules, and they not only served to entertain spectators with athletic prowess but also embraced a religious connection.

Archaeological Museum, Crete

A Minoan boxer, circa 1700 B.C. Owing to the small gloves used at this time, the boxers wore helmets to protect their heads.

Wrestling and pugilism, in particular, were quite popular during this time. In Crete, wrestlers wore a special helmet with cheek guards, while boxers fought with their heads uncovered. Both, however, had elaborate hairstyles and wore girdles, sandals and necklaces. The importance of Cretan boxing is even more significant in the Aegean Islands. Evidence of this is found in a fresco from the second millennium B.C. uncovered in Thera. Presented on a black steatite rhyton from Hagia Triada (See Page 33.) are boxing contests in three of its four carved bands, depicting the process of victory of one athlete over another. Two youths are boxing, using the same equipment favored in Crete. They wear metal helmets that protect the face and head, leaving but a narrow opening for their eyes; boxing gloves are worn, but only on their right hands. The winner, consumed by excitement, is shown having delivered the decisive blow as the vanquished is sinking to his knees, shielding his face.

Athletics developed rapidly in the Mycenaean period with improved techniques and the addition of new events. This development can be attributed to the general character of Mycenaean society, which was warlike in nature. Boxing and wrestling passed into mainland Greece from Crete and became the most popular sports in the Mycenaean world.

The continuation and survival of the Mycenaean tradition is traced primarily in the *Iliad* (the story of the Trojan War) and the *Odyssey* (the adventures of the Greek hero Odysseus in the years following the war); both of Homer's epic poems attest to the love of competition that dominated Greek life during that period. Young men aspired to intense physical effort, and heroes competed to excel before the crowds. This point in time, called the Geometric period, was characterized by both heroic ideals and a genuine sporting spirit.

Among the many contests described in the *Iliad* were the funeral games held in honor of the deceased Patroklos, which featured the combat sports of boxing, wrestling and *hoplomachia* (armed contest). Prizes were awarded by Achilles to both the victors and the vanquished, and they included beautiful slaves skilled in some craft, horses, oxen, mules, cauldrons, cups, gold and iron. The games took place before the entire army, near the tomb of Patroklos.

Following the chariot race, a boxing match was held, featuring the competitors Epeios and Euryalos. As they did in Crete, they wore loincloths and had leather strips wrapped around their hands. Epeios quickly defeated his rival with a blow to the face that knocked him to the ground. In a gesture of good sportsmanship, he was equally as quick to help the opposing fighter to his feet. A wrestling match was next. This combative sport required more proficiency than boxing, with the winner decided by successfully throwing his opponent to the ground. In this contest, the superior skill of Odysseus was matched by the immense might of Ajax. Because neither could throw the other, Ajax, confident in his strength, proposed that they should try to lift one another. In the first attempt by Ajax, a strong blow to the back of the knee by Odysseus caused both men to fall to the ground. Odysseus then took his turn but he only succeeded in moving Ajax slightly. He then placed his knee between the legs of his foe, which resulted in only a minor loss of balance. Achilles, realizing that neither competitor had the advantage, declared a draw and divided the prizes equally.

Unquestionably, the most dangerous contest described in the *Iliad* was the hoplomachia. This was a fierce duel in which opponents competed while dressed in full armor and attempted to wound the other. Ajax and Diomedes were the participants and began by rushing each other three times without finding their mark. On the next attack, however, Diomedes' weapon was about to pierce the throat of Ajax when the spectators, fearing fatal consequences, intervened and called for the bout to cease.

Although the Homeric poems describe the games as an outlet for the athletic heroes to display their excellence and intense desire for victory, they also emphasize the spirit of good sportsmanship. There is no evidence in his writings that the will to win gave way to the use of force, in the combat events or any other competitions. The ideal hero, according to Homer, possessed physical and mental strength and was intelligent and courageous. Only the "best men" took part in the games, a view expressed by Homer that was often taken to mean that sport was a prerogative of the aristocracy. But from the Geometric period onward, participation in the games was not the exclusive privilege of the "best men" as is documented in the *Odyssey*. These athletes were not famous heroes but figures from social life. For the Phaiakians, the mighty seafaring people mentioned in the *Odyssey*, the most essential factors in competition were in simply pursuing victory and imposing one's full effort. Prizes were not given, the athlete's reward being the satisfaction of being first. This attitude set the groundwork for the high athletic ideal of Greece's Classical period.

In Homeric Greek, the term *agon* symbolized rivalry of sport and the martial combat of war, both of which were, in a sense, considered to be games. Two key points stand out in the mighty Homeric world: the value of systematic practice among the athletes, and the high esteem that Homeric society attached to sports competition. This is evident in his lengthy poems that became Greece's treasured epics. In the *Iliad*, all the leaders of the army competed. The Phaiakians believed that even wealth was secondary to what a man could achieve by his hands and feet. The competitive spirit elevated man beyond the realm of daily life to that of high ideals, making its athletes heroes.

Even in the poetic works of Hesiod, which were somewhat different from that of Homer, sport is interwoven with the joys of a peaceful life. In his poem *Works and Days*, Hesiod focused on the two Strifes, a representation of good against evil. The first seduced men into war and destruction, while the second encouraged creative competition and progress. In *The Shield*, he described the shield of Herakles, presenting two sides of the city in times of war and peace. In the peaceful city, alongside scenes of the harvest and the vintage, there are sporting images of contests including wrestling and boxing.

5. THE PANHELLENIC GAMES

The gods were worshipped by the Greeks in religious ceremonies called *festivals*, which commemorated some significant mythical tradition or some act by a god. They included funeral processions, sacrifices and athletic contests. Each city-state arranged numerous local festivals, but all joined in honoring their greatest gods in four major events. These became known as the Panhellenic (all-Greek) festivals and consisted of the Olympics, the Pythian games, the Isthmian games and the Nemean games.

The combat athletes competed for victory and a crown of wild olive. Their ultimate goal, however, was for something far greater: fame, and the respect of their countrymen throughout Hellas. Although all free men were encouraged to participate, the Spartans elected not to take part in the pankration event. They preferred to hold their own local festivals, which allowed them the freedom to play an even more brutal version of the sport that allowed eye gouging and biting.

The tradition of honoring dead heroes with funerary games was followed throughout antiquity. Alexander the Great preserved this tradition by organizing games after each one of his victories to express his gratitude to the gods and to honor the fallen. Just as Achilles honored his dead friend, Patroclus, with games, Alexander did for his deceased friend, Hephaistion, by arranging a major competition in Babylon that attracted 3,000 competitors.

THE OLYMPIC GAMES

The Olympic Games were dedicated to Zeus, the greatest of the gods, and were held every four years at his sanctuary in Olympia. Legend has it that they were founded either by Herakles, Pelops or Zeus (in celebration of defeating Kronos in wrestling for world sovereignty). According to the ancient tradition, the gods and heroes were the first to compete in the Olympics, serving as models for mortals who continued the games until the late Roman period.

The games were celebrated in midsummer, which was evidenced by the suffering of both spectators and athletes from the unbearable heat and the large number of flies and mosquitoes. Aelian told the story of the miller of Chios, who threatened his slave that he would send him to Olympia to follow the games if his lackluster effort in grinding corn persisted. He thought it was more exhausting to roast in the hot sun watching the events than to grind corn in the mill.

Official records of Olympian champions were kept starting in 776 B.C., by which time the magnitude of the games attracted the interest of all throughout Greece. All free-born Greeks (with the exception of women) were entitled to compete. The games were first overseen by the Eleans (the people of Elis—the general region of Olympia) and later by the Pisans, until the Eleans, with Spartan support, won back control around 580 B.C.

The divine-heroic model was the basis for the primary events at classic Olympia. The assimilation of mortals with the gods who founded the games was the mission of the sanctuary of Olympia, as it was with other Greek sanctuaries. Their lessons were spiritual, in the sense that the contest was the best means by which man could awaken and develop the vast mental and physical powers endowed to him by nature. The games in the sanctuary were not merely a spectacle but a religious ritual. The champions of these contests were worshipped like heroes in their native cities after their deaths, enjoying the same adulation as the first mythical victors. Victory in the games was the highest honor a Greek could ever aspire to attain. "Only the brazen heaven is inaccessible to him," Pindar stated about the Olympic winner Phrikias of Thessaly.

For the Greeks, the highest cultivation of the physical, spiritual and intellectual capabilities of man was also the predominant theme for its educational system. No other culture before or after the Greeks ever set for themselves such a lofty goal. And for no other people did the prize for this ideal, the crown of victory, become the most gratifying award that the gods could bestow on mortals. Competition was fundamental to the continued evolution of Greek culture. It was responsible for every significant achievement in athletics, art, politics and every other aspect of life.

In the earliest years, the contests took place on a single day and had only two events: wrestling and a footrace that consisted of one lap around the stadium. By 471 B.C., the number of contests had increased to 18, which lengthened the games to five days. They were organized by assigned officials responsible for the training of the athletes and the enforcement of the rules of each competition. The opening day consisted of customary oaths and sacrifices to the gods. The events took up the remaining days, with the combat events standing out as the most popular and spectacular among the spectators. Wrestling was the first of these, having been entered in the 18th Olympiad of 708 B.C., with boxing (*pyx*) added in the 23rd Olympiad of 688 B.C., and the brutal pankration in the 33rd Olympics of 648 B.C. Of these, pankration was considered the ultimate test of an athlete's strength, stamina and skill.

On the final day of the games, the winners were crowned, receiving the prize of the *cotinus* (a wreath made from an olive branch) and money. The names of the champions were inscribed on stone pillars in recognition of their triumphs, and they were treated like heroes and honored by their cities after returning home.

The games were of immense political and social significance, attracting the most influential people of Greece as both spectators and competitors. Respected statesmen invested great sums of money to build chariot teams to compete, and famous writers, such as Herodotus and Empedocles, gave readings at the games. The religious fervor and aristocratic pride of the Olympic spirit can be found in Pindar's *Victory Odes*.

Unity and peace, both important aspirations of the Greek world, were realized within the sanctuaries, especially at Olympia. Perhaps the most striking aspect of the Olympics was the Olympic Truce, which was announced by heralds in all major provinces of mainland Greece months before the start of each festival. Wars came to a standstill in honor of the truce. During the Peloponnesian War, for example, visitors from enemy cities coexisted peacefully during the games to ensure safe passage for the thousands of competitors, spectators and religious pilgrims in attendance.

Violators were severely punished. In 420 B.C., the Spartans were banned from competing after their assault on Elean territory shortly after the truce was declared. To enforce the ban, several thousand troops from enemy cities of Sparta guarded Olympia. A more notorious truce-breaking occurred in 364 B.C., when a conflict was waged in the sanctuary itself by the Pisans and Arcadians against the Eleans. In the same century, Macedonia's King Alexander (later called "the Great") was obliged to pay damages to an Athenian pilgrim who had been robbed en route to Olympia by some of the renowned king's troops.

Within the sanctuary of Olympia, the Greeks became aware of their spiritual unity and overcame the differences between them. Naturally, Olympia did not achieve complete political unification, but it embraced something that Greece considered even more relevant: the commonality of the Greek spirit, which was held in the highest regard despite the opposition, rivalry and fragmentation of the Greeks in their isolated and hostile cities.

It was at Olympia and other sanctuaries that the heroes of Thermopylae, Marathon and Salamis were formed. Even the victory of Greece over the Persians is represented as an Olympic victory. This is evidenced in the first Olympiad following the Persian wars circa 476 B.C.—possibly the happiest moment in the history of Greece and the most exciting in the history of the sanctuary. Not only was the Greeks' faith restored in the gods and in the ideal of competition between free men, but it also became greater than ever before. Themistokles, the main architect of the victory, was cheered in the stadium like an Olympic victor, and the spectators paid more attention to him than to the competitors.

THE PYTHIAN GAMES

The Pythian games were considered the second most prestigious of the great religious sports festivals of the ancient Greek world, after the Olympics. They began around the sixth century B.C., soon after Apollo, the god of music, killed the terrible serpent Python, and they took place at his holiest shrine, Delphi. The events focused primarily on music and drama competitions, and they included singers, lyre players and choruses. The games were initially staged every eight years, although the schedule was later changed to every four years. Sports contests were added in 582 B.C. and were attended by all the city-states, confirming their popularity. These events were modeled after those held at Olympia and followed the same program. Laurel crowns were awarded to the champions (the laurel tree was sacred to Apollo), along with the same honors and privileges that athletic victors received.

THE ISTHMIAN GAMES

According to Athenian myth, the Isthmian games were founded during the early 500s B.C. by the hero Theseus, in emulation of Herakles' establishment of the Olympics. They took place in his honor every two years in the sanctuary of Poseidon near Corinth. The structure of the events was much like that of the Olympics. The combat sports were among the crowd favorites, although contests in music and painting were also included. Winners were given wreaths of pine twigs and, for a short time, garlands of wild celery (an influence of the Nemean games).

THE NEMEAN GAMES

Dedicated to Zeus, the games at Nemea were established as a Panhellenic festival in 573 B.C. and were held every two years. They were also patterned after the Olympic Games and featured combat sports, including pankration. The Nemean games became more celebrated in Argos than in Nemea because, according to myth, it was there that Herakles instituted the games after slaying the Nemean lion—the first of his Twelve Labors. The presiding *hellano-dikai* (judges) were dressed in black in a symbol of mourning for the dead son of Nemean King Lycurgus (hence the term "funeral games") and awarded crowns of wild celery to the victorious contestants. Although the Nemean games were considered the least important of the Panhellenic games, they were nonetheless attended by large numbers of famous athletes.

COMPETITIVE RULES

The Eleans, more than other Greeks, promoted interest in the games, and they were able to accomplish this by strict adherence to the rules and by their impartial verdicts. This was the rationale behind assembling the hellanodikai for 10 months in order to train them. All Greeks religiously respected and followed the rules, and Pindar described those regulations observed in the Olympic Games as the "laws of Zeus."

One such rule applied to the age of those competing. The Eleans were careful to distinguish the men's games from the boys' division. It therefore became the decision of the hellanodikai to divide the athletes into specified age groups, and their right to accept or to reject them was unrestricted. They selected the category in which any youth between the ages of 12 and 18 would compete on the basis of his appearance. Once a competitor was admitted into the games, he was not allowed to withdraw. The day before the 201st Olympiad, a pankration entrant named Sarapion of Alexandria became fearful of his opponent and secretly left Olympia. He was fined and appears to be the only recorded athlete punished for this reason up until the second century.

Another rule involved the *ephedreia* (the bye). In wrestling, boxing and pankration, the contestants were drawn to compete in pairs, but one competitor would occasionally be left without an opponent. Instead of being excluded from the contest, he would compete with the ultimate victor. Called the *ephedros* (man in waiting), he would, in a sense, be the lucky man in the draw because he was fresh while his opponent was fatigued from his previous matches.

It was also possible for an athlete to be proclaimed the winner without competing. The Greeks called this *akoniti*—a win without actually beating an opponent. Although Philostratos stated that the Eleans recognized an akoniti victory only in wrestling, there is much evidence that shows otherwise. In the 75th Olympiad (480 B.C.), Theagenes of Thasos had entered the boxing and pankration events. After defeating his boxing opponent, Euthymos, Theagenes was too tired to continue and withdrew, thinking that his pankration opponent, Dromeus, would not be awarded the crown because the law stated that the akoniti decision was upheld only in wrestling. The hellanodikai, however, gave the victory to Dromeus, making him the first akoniti victor at the Olympic Games. In addition, Theagenes was fined and was not allowed to partake in the boxing competitions at the next two Olympiads, thereby allowing Euthymos to win.

Similar to the akoniti was the *hiera* (sacred) decision. This applied when a bout ended in a draw, in which case the victory was offered to the god in the sanctuary. An inscription from the early second century describes the *pankratiast* Rufus as having fought until the stars filled the heavens, yet he was neither victorious nor vanquished.

Penalties for violating the rules were imposed by the hellanodikai, and there were three types: fines, exclusion from the games and corporal punishment. Flogging was one of the lighter penalties and was employed for minor infractions. The money collected from the fines went in part to the sanctuary of the god, as well as to the wronged opponent if there was one. Perhaps the greatest fine was levied against the Spartans for their capture of two small towns, Lepreon and Phyrkon, during the Olympic Truce. The Eleans not only fined the Spartans but also proposed that Lepreon be returned to them, to which the Spartans pleaded ignorance that the truce had been in effect. In response to their refusal, the Eleans excluded them from the games, and they finally agreed to evacuate Lepreon and pay the god's share of the fine.

The fines were paid without question by violators of the rules, for they realized the severity of the sanctions. If the athlete was unable to pay, the responsibility was assumed by his city to avoid exclusion from the games. The revenue from the fines was used to make statues of Zeus, called "zanes," on which engraved verses declared that an Olympic victory should be won not by money or unacceptable means but by speed and strength.

Although the national festivals of Greece tended to have uniform rules, those of local contests undoubtedly varied. *The Classical Review and Papers of the American School of Classical Studies of Athens* describes inscriptions discovered in the village of Fassiler in Pisidia during the second century. They state that the pankratiasts "are not to use sand to dust themselves like wrestlers, nor are they to use wrestling, but to be content with upright hitting." This might mean that grappling was not allowed, neither standing nor on the ground, only fighting with bare hands and feet. It was further stipulated that, after winning a prize, a competitor could not compete again on the same day. If a slave was successful, he had to surrender a quarter of his prize money to the other competitors.

THE OFFICIALS

During the Mythical period, the individual who awarded the prizes was also the judge in the games. Iphitos, the legendary Elean king, solely supervised their conduct. In the 50th Olympiad, there were two *agonothetai* (or hellanodikai, as they later became known), but by the 75th Olympiad, the number increased to nine, of whom three judged the combat events. From that time onward, the number of hellanodikai varied according to the fluctuating fortunes of the state of Elis. Beginning with the 108th Olympic Games in 348 B.C., however, the number of hellanodikai was firmly fixed at 10, and it remained this way until they were abolished in Greece. Originally, the hellanodikai title was hereditary and held for life, although after 584 B.C., the members were chosen by lot among Elean citizens. They held office for one Olympiad and were formally trained for 10 months. During their stay in Elis, the hellanodikai were instructed in the duties and the regulations governing the conduct of the games by the *nomophylakes* (observers of the laws). One month before the games, they followed the athletes' training and made their selections as to who would take part.

The hellanodikai donned purple cloaks during the games and had great freedom in the exercise of their duties. They inflicted both fines and physical punishment, and they could prevent athletes from competing. They also awarded the prizes, and their verdicts were respected without any possibility of being overturned. If any athlete believed that he was the victim of an unjust decision, he had recourse with the Elean Council, which had the power to penalize a *hellanodikes* for a poor judgment but did not have the authority to invalidate or overturn it.

The hellanodikai were assisted in their tasks by the *alytai* (special police officers), who were responsible for the event's smooth operation, and the *mastigophoroi* (scourge bearers) and the *rabdouchoi* (rod bearers) played an important part in the execution of the alytai's decisions. In addition to these officials, Olympia was served during the games by the following staff: the *theekolos* (priests); the *manteis*, who provided the oracle responses; the *exegetes*, who explained to foreigners the rituals of the games; the *auletes*, who played the flute during the sacrifices; the *xyleus*, who supplied the poplar wood for the sacrifices; the *grammateus*, who announced the names of the competitors; the *spondaules*, who supplied the rhythmic accompaniments for the libations and sacrifices; the *epispondorchestai* and *hypospondorchestai*, who made certain the treaties were observed; and the *kathemerothytes*, who carried out the daily animal sacrifices.

6. COMBAT SPORT IN POETRY AND ART

The Panhellenic combat athletes, especially those who were Olympian victors, were honored in recognition of their success. They were treated like heroes and received official receptions after returning home, and they often held high office positions or were appointed generals or leaders of colonies. Those from Sparta enjoyed the privilege of being included in the *homoioi* (the equals), which entitled them to fight in war at the side of the king. To ensure a victor's immortality, he was enshrined in poetry and art. Pindar believed that, of the two forms of expression, the former was more suitable for preserving one's legendary status. Even though it stood in the sacred sanctuaries of Zeus, a statue was immobile, and one's accomplishments and prowess could only be familiar to those who chanced to pass by and read the inscription in the stone pillars. The odes, on the other hand, would reach every corner of the Greek world.

An example of this occurred in 485 B.C., when a youth from Aigina won the pankration event at the Nemean games and sought out Pindar to compose a victory ode for him. When his representatives learned they would be charged a fee of 3,000 drachmas, they decided to order a bronze statue of the youth for the same cost. Later, they changed their minds and commissioned the choral poet, who used the outset of his ode to defend his craft. He wrote:

> I am no maker of images, not one to fashion idols standing quiet on pedestals. Take ship of burden, rather, or boat, delight of my song forth from Aigina, scattering the news that Lampon's son, Pytheas, has won the garland of success at Nemea, pankratiast, showing not yet on his cheeks the summer of life to bring soft blossoming.

The Greek combat athlete, realizing he was mortal, had a great desire to ensure that his memory was kept alive. And of all the accolades one might receive, only two could make this possible: the statue and literary works of art. If he was not wealthy enough to afford both, one was obligated to choose. Many would think that a statue made of marble or bronze would certainly outlast words written on papyrus. However, through the years, natural disasters caused marble to crumble and bronze to melt. In contrast, nearly 60 victory odes survived to the present day, thus reaffirming Pindar's belief that the word endures longer than deeds in one's lifetime.

It is chiefly through the literary works that escaped destruction that the proficiency of the ancient Greek wrestlers, boxers and pankratiasts was admired throughout the centuries. The very nature of the written word, with its great resourcefulness of expression, has paid tribute to their skill. For this reason, it is the victory ode that helps us to understand that the Greeks viewed a champion at the Panhellenic competitions as manifesting his moral character through his athletic achievement, bringing honor to his family and country, and glorifying the gods who had helped him secure victory.

For the athlete, the demands of training his body and of competing in Hellenic combat sport, particularly pankration, derived its greatest value from being created and governed by the gods themselves. In its praise of the victor and his ancestors, the victory ode compared the feat of the mortal with that of an ancient hero, uniting gods and man. Plato believed that it was human nature to crave immortality and that for the ancient Greek this yearning was even more intense because his religion did not promise an afterlife. A victor at the games had the benefit of having his name and achievements preserved for generations by a statue or by the victory ode that perpetuated his *kleos*—his immortal glory.

Fighting and combat sport were so ingrained in ancient Greek culture that even the holy walls of the Parthenon were decorated with fight scenes. The *metopes* (sculptures) of the Parthenon represented various struggles between the forces of order and justice and of criminal chaos: on the west side, the mythical battle against the Amazons; on the south, the battle between the Lapiths and the centaurs; on the east, the battle between the gods and the giants; on the north, the Greeks versus the Trojans. In Hellenistic art, thousands of sport scenes and athletes are represented in Attic vase paintings alone. It is interesting to note the direction taken by the athletic ideal at the end of the Greek world as mirrored by this expressionism. The boxer depicted by Athenian artist Apollonios in the first century B.C. demonstrates this in striking fashion. The boxer appears inhumanly tough and disfigured, and he is resting his fearsome limbs following a fatal contest. The horrid gloves worn on his hands add to his powerful, intimidating presence. As combat sport became increasingly violent, the competitors were further removed from their original beauty; the aesthetics of the naked Greek athlete gave way to those of a more brutal combatant known as the gladiator.

Delphi Archaeological Museum

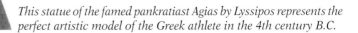

This statue of the famed pankratiast Agias by Lyssipos represents the perfect artistic model of the Greek athlete in the 4th century B.C.

PART II
EVOLUTION,
FROM ALPHA TO OMEGA

Greek myth contains hundreds of stories from the Heroic Age. Among the most popular is the *Odyssey*, an epic poem narrated by the sightless Homer that describes the 10-year homeward wanderings of the wily and resourceful Greek hero Odysseus, king of Ithaca, following the Trojan War and the fall of Troy. The Greek martial way has taken a similar journey, having come full circle from the time stretching before Plato (the alpha) into the 21st century (the omega).

7. COMBAT METHODS OF ANTIQUITY

BATTLEFIELD PANKRATION (PAMMACHON)

During the Mycenaean period (1600 B.C. to 1100 B.C.), warfare was considered heroic. Those who achieved success on the battlefield were glorified (or even deified) in their homelands. The exploits of these men are aptly described in both the *Iliad* and the *Odyssey*. When the individual warrior lost the opportunity to distinguish his name in combat, competitions were devised to simulate combat in order to attain fame.

When combat sports were established as part of the Hellenic culture, the greatest military leaders disapproved of them from the outset. Alexander the Great, Plato, Xenophon and Epaminondas all voiced their discord against the practical utility of boxing and pankration. Their objections stemmed from the fact that, while the purpose of war was to kill the opponent, the purpose of combat sport was to defeat him with a minimum of permanent injury. To them, warfare demanded good technique and timing, whereas sport was primarily size- and strength-dependent. This was particularly true in ancient times when there were no weight divisions.

For combat sport to be acceptable, it had to be applicable as a training method for what the soldier might expect to face on the battlefield. Homer wrote about the difference between combat sport and life-or-death fighting in his description of the champion pugilist Epeios, who asked that his incompetence on the battlefield be excused owing to his boxing awards. Plato maintained that the groundwork of the pankratiast was ineffective for war and that all combat athletes were overtrained and overspecialized. For these reasons, he believed they had no place in his ideal state.

While Plato had strong misgivings about the fighting efficiency of the athletes of his day, he did recommend wrestling for training the youth, not so much for competition but for mock warfare. In *The Republic*, his "athlete of war" addresses such training. Euripides was yet another critic who belittled the combat athletes:

> What outstanding wrestler or expert at punching the jaw of another has done his ancestral homeland a service by winning a crown? Do they fight by kicking through shields with their feet expelling the country's enemies? No one standing next to steel indulges in this stupidity.

The system of unarmed-fighting skills employed in warfare was not specifically called pankration but was referred to as *pammachon* (total fight). Used primarily on the blood-soaked grounds of battle, pammachon is not to be confused with the Olympic sport because no other Greeks (with the exception of the ultramilitant Spartans) wanted to "play" this game. Pankration was an athletic contest in which one fought for the glorious cotinus. Pammachon was simply an art of killing. Although honor was the common thread in both, there was no taking of a crown or prisoners on the battlefield.

HOPLOMACHIA (ARMED COMBAT)

Hoplomachia was a contest between two competitors wearing heavy armor consisting of a shield, breastplate, helmet and greaves (leg armor). Their weapons consisted of a spear and sword. Normally, the spear was used along with a small round shield and sometimes with a large rectangular shield called a *thyreos*. Held in the Hellenistic period, hoplomachia competitions were essentially exhibitions of skill in weaponry, agility and physical endurance (especially considering the weight of the armor). The hoplomachia was primarily a ritualistic re-enactment of hand-to-hand combat honoring either a distinguished dead warrior or someone whose life had been taken in war. The event was intended to simulate warfare and consisted of mock duels that bore no relation to the bloody armed battles of the Roman arenas that emerged later.

Armed combat competition was closely connected with the changes in military tactics and the manner in which Greek youths were raised in the early part of the fourth century B.C. Professional trainers during this time held a prominent position in the gymnasia and were well paid for teaching armed combat as an art.

Madrid National Archaeological Museum

Hoplomachia was an exhibition of skill between two heavily armored opponents.

ARMS AND ARMOR

Before the establishment of the Olympics, military strategy was refined and the value of the individual warrior paled before the armed might of the organized infantry unit. More important to the *hoplite* (foot soldier) than empty-hand skills was his ability to fight with arms and armor. His role was cardinal in warfare, and the hoplite owed much to his defensive armor in particular.

Modern literature tells us that the early hoplite was named after his innovative war shield, called the *hoplon*, which was round, heavy (about 16 pounds) and about 3 feet in diameter. It was held by a handgrip and a bronze armband around the forearm. Painted on the shield were animals and mythological creatures; the Gorgon's head was particularly popular. Notoriously difficult to hold for a long duration, the cumbersome shield was almost always dropped by a hoplite fleeing from battle. For the Spartans, maintaining possession of one's shield meant keeping your honor. This was reflected in a mother's proverbial command to her son who was leaving for war: "Return with your shield or upon it."

The hoplite's head was protected by a bronze helmet. This could be pulled forward in battle to shade his face (it featured eye slits and breathing spaces for the nose and mouth), or it could be pushed to the back of the head, leaving the face uncovered. Helmets were often decorated with natural horsehair crests. Black, white or even multicolored crests were also used.

The hoplite's body was protected by numerous layers of canvas glued together and reinforced with metal scales. Because his shield did not protect the hoplite below the knees, his lower legs were protected by a pair of bronze greaves. The hoplite's chief offensive weapon was a spear that was up to 9 feet in length. Unlike earlier spears, this was tipped with iron and was used only for thrusting, not for throwing. He also carried a *xiphos*—a straight, double-bladed sword made of iron and bronze. The xiphos was about 2 feet long and was suitable for cut-

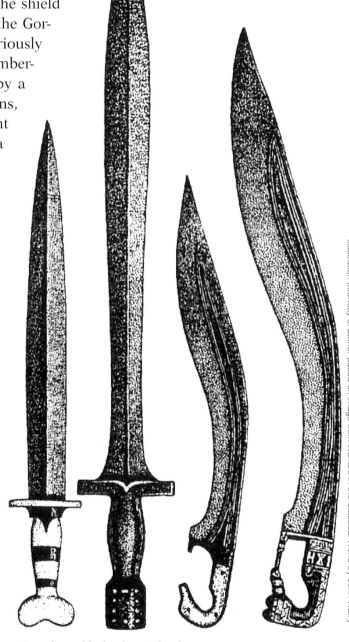

Swords used by hoplites in battle.

Illustration courtesy of author based on image from *Warfare in the Classical World* by John Warry

ting and thrusting. It was ideal for close combat and extremely lethal in the hands of a trained Spartan infantryman. An alternative sword, called a *kopis*, was a heavy single-edged weapon used for close-quarters combat. It was short, convex in shape and used for slashing and chopping. The hoplite also carried a dagger, or *parazone*, on his belt. This was a vital accessory and served as both a last-resort weapon as well as a utility knife. Other ancient Greek weaponry included the *sagaris* (battle ax), *kopidian* (curved slashing knife) and the *xyele* (sickle).

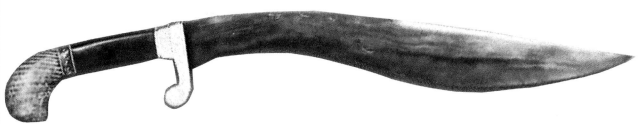

The hoplite's kopis, which was used for close-quarters fighting.

Strategically, a hoplite did not normally fight alone; he was trained and equipped to stand, charge and do battle side by side with his comrades in an orderly, multiranked formation. The hoplite relied mainly on his spear, which he thrust overhand at the enemy while shielding himself from their spears, and the sword came into play if the lance was broken or lost. On warships, hoplites served as "marines" and were armed with javelins (for throwing). Those who fell overboard quickly drowned, the weight of their armor pulling them to the bottom of the sea.

His heavy armor did not make the warrior invulnerable. Because it did not cover his neck, groin or thighs, deadly wounds to these areas were common, as were fatal blows to the head. Sometimes the helmets and breastplates were pierced, which was evidenced by the recently recovered remains of a Spartan hoplite who was buried with an iron spear point lodged deep inside his chest. The terrain on which the hoplites waged combat was also important; level ground was preferable to hills, which often shattered the hoplites' formation, leaving them open to attacks from lightly armed skirmishers.

It was always possible that the hoplite could lose hold of his spear and sword and would have to rely on hand-to-hand fighting, but because strikes and kicks could not penetrate armor, unarmed tactics revolved more around grappling skills. Unbalancing the enemy soldier and bringing him to the ground, where he could be disposed of with a short bladed weapon, was the backup plan when one's spear and sword were rendered useless. This strategy was similar to the *kumiuchi* skills employed by the warriors in feudal Japan.

Hoplite armies were initially made up of citizens who could afford the cost of a panoply if his city went to war. In states governed by oligarchies, one had to be at least of hoplite status to be admitted as a citizen. Professional soldiers also were recruited for service; the Athenian Xenophon is perhaps the most noted mercenary in Hellenic history, having marched deep into the Persian Empire in 401 B.C. in service of a rebel Persian prince.

From the early sixth century B.C. into Roman times, the Greeks came to rely on the *phalanx*, a tactical battle formation in which the heavily armed hoplites formed tight ranks at least eight men deep while using overlapping shields for protection. They also carried 14-foot spikes that they thrust with great force at their enemies as they marched forward. Because other infantrymen of the day were armed only with shorter, 6- to 8-foot jabbing spears, the phalanx offered an advantage. The proper deployment of the phalanx involved a coordinated effort with lightly armed infantry to guard its unshielded right flank and chase off enemy projectile troops. The prime function of the phalanx in combat was defensive in nature, holding the enemies' charge and damaging their formation while the cavalry looked for a weak point to attack.

Though militaristic combat certainly focused more on the strategies of armed warfare during this period, various historical records show that pankration training played a significant role in a hoplite's preparation. It is evident that pankration was basic to the soldiers who served under Alexander the Great during his Asian conquests in 326 B.C., as well as to those who served under other famed commanders.

Philostratos maintained that the great combat athletes of the past engaged in "war training for sport and sport training for war." He pointed out that the Spartans first developed boxing for military use. Their soldiers were not protected by helmets but only by a shield, and boxing enabled them to practice parrying blows directed to the head, as well as to withstand the force of those that did find their mark. He also wrote of the Greeks' discovery of the military effectiveness of both pankration and wrestling at the Battle of Marathon, where empty-hand combat became necessary when soldiers lost their spears and swords. But perhaps the most striking example of pankration's effectiveness in military conflict took place in 480 B.C. during the Persian Wars. In the Battle of Thermopylae, the Spartan King Leonides blocked King Xerxes' Persian army of perhaps 200,000 with only 5,000 Greek soldiers.

For the first two days of this historic battle, the Persians failed to advance through the narrow mountain pass and they sustained heavy losses. But with the help of a traitorous Greek named Ephialtes, the Persians discovered a footpath that enabled their troops to attack from behind Greek lines. Leonides, after learning that he was outflanked, sent most of the army south to safety. However, he and his royal guard of 300 Spartans remained to face the incredible odds. Once the battle resumed, they fought fearlessly until their spears and swords were broken. Those who were unarmed continued to battle, employing their pankration strikes, throws and chokes with lethal efficiency. Many enemy soldiers had their eyes gouged out, their necks broken or were strangled to death.

When Leonides was killed, he was some distance away from his forces. Some of the Spartans formed a tight group, fought their way to his body, picked it up and fought their way back to the main group on a small hill, where they made their final stand. The Persians demanded the body of Leonides in return for the Spartans' lives, but the men refused to abandon their king. In the end, however, the numbers proved to be too much, and the remaining troops were killed by a hail of spears and arrows. Although, in military terms, Thermopylae was a Greek failure, the battle became very significant in the sense of patriotism and spirit. Like other suicidal exploits, the Spartan defense at Thermopylae inspired a strong belief in the Hellenic mind and also brought respect to the weaponless pankration tactics that had been in question.

Illustration by Clive Spong

A hoplite, circa 500 B.C.

8. THE HEAVY EVENTS

The "heavy events" referred to the three combat sports of the Panhellenic games: wrestling, boxing and pankration. The term was given to these contests because they not only were the crowd favorites but also were the domain of the larger, heavier athlete. Bouts in the boys' division took place on the second day of the Olympic schedule, while the men's matches took place on the fourth day.

The contests of the heavy events were elimination tournaments with pairings of opponents made by drawing lots from a silver urn sacred to Zeus. On these bean-size lots were inscriptions of alpha, beta, gamma and so forth, and they were drawn by each athlete following a prayer to Zeus. A *mastigophoros* (whip bearer) stood next to each competitor and held his hand closed, not allowing him to know the letter he selected. The hellanodikai would formally announce the matchups by the letters in sequence.

In the event of an odd number of competitors, there could be a bye in several rounds. In extremely large tournaments, there could be as many as nine rounds of contests. Many victory odes describe a single athlete defeating four opponents in a single day. The winners of each bout faced one another until only two remained for the finals. To avoid a "no-decision," bouts were allowed to continue for some time. Even then, if a clear winner was not decided, the victor's wreath was dedicated to the god and not to the competitors.

The contestants entered the arena in the accepted Greek manner: totally nude and heavily oiled. They proceeded to pay homage to Zeus and saluted the officials and one another. The hellanodikes then commanded the bout to commence and the fighters engaged in fierce battle.

WRESTLING

Wrestling is Greece's oldest combat sport, and it had immense appeal in Hellenistic society. Philostratos claimed that Palaistra, the daughter of Hermes, invented wrestling and that the entire world rejoiced at the discovery because "the iron weapons of war would be cast aside and the stadia would gain sweeter glory than the military camps." He also emphasized the practical effectiveness of wrestling in warfare by claiming that the military achievement at Marathon was almost a wrestling contest and that the Spartans at Thermopylae employed their bare hands after losing their spears and swords. Plutarch attributed the victory at Leuktra to the supreme wrestling skills of the Thebans and the Boiotians during that period.

The art of wrestling was believed to have been refined by Theseus, when he wrestled and killed Kerkyon. Pausanias wrote, "Only size and might mattered until Theseus introduced the qualities needed by a good wrestler: strength and a great build." The academic philosopher Poleman attributed the discovery of wrestling to Theseus' trainer, Phorbas of Athens. The historian Istros contended that Theseus was taught wrestling by the goddess Athena. Other "inventors" of the sport include Hermes and Peleus, who grappled with Atalanta in the funeral games honoring King Pelias, and Herakles, who defeated Antaios, Acheloos and Triton in wrestling contests.

The first wrestling champion in the men's division at Olympia was Eurybatos of Sparta in 708 B.C. A boy's category was added in 632 B.C. The rules of the sport were said to have been first established by Orikadmos, an early Sicilian wrestler. Striking, grabbing the groin and

Atalanta and Peleus grapple at the games in honor of the dead King Pelias.

Antikensammlungen, Munich

biting were not allowed. If the wrestlers went out of bounds, the referee halted the contest and returned them to the center of the pit, where they resumed with the same hold they had when the match was interrupted.

Wrestling was an independent event at the Panhellenic games but was also part of the pentathlon. There were two forms of the sport: *orthia pale* (upright wrestling) and *kato pale* (ground wrestling). In the first, the object was to throw one's opponent to the ground; in the second, a throw was not enough, and the contest continued until a competitor admitted defeat and was compelled to withdraw. Holds, including submissions, were freely used, and the event was similar to pankration, except there was no striking. An athlete withdrew only when he was so completely exhausted that he could resist no longer.

A wrestler lifts his opponent with a waist lock.

For competitions in the stadium, a minimum of five and a maximum of eight pairs of wrestlers were chosen. In order for one to gain victory in upright wrestling, he had to throw his opponent to the ground three times. It was not necessary to pin an opponent or make him submit. The rules required that a wrestler cleanly throw his opponent to the ground and either remain standing or fall on top of him. If any part of the body came in contact with the ground, even a knee, it was counted as a fall.

There were two areas in the palaistra to practice the two wrestling styles. Upright wrestling was conducted in the sand, while ground wrestling was usually held on wet soil. The mud stuck to the bodies of the competitors, making them slippery and holds difficult to apply. In upright wrestling, the upper part of the body—the neck, shoulders, arms, chest and waist—received the most attention in training sessions. In ground wrestling, the arms, waist, thighs and knees were developed most.

Greek artwork reveals that ancient wrestling techniques were sophisticated—perhaps as sophisticated as the grappling systems of today. Most of the depicted scenes focus on the upright aspect of the contest, for reasons of the conventional nature of vase paintings and

Florence Archaeological Museum

The fall was often obtained with highly developed throwing techniques, such as the shoulder throw.

for aesthetic preference; Greek artisans preferred upright scenes because they fit better on vases, which were more vertical as opposed to wide. They also believed that more of the physique and the beauty of the athletes' muscularity could be painted with the athletes standing instead of prone. Plato thought stand-up skills, especially the execution of a clean decisive throw, formed the purest element of the sport.

A wrestling contest would generally start with the participants clinching each other's necks or attempting to control one another's wrists. Frequently, their heads would press against each other, in what might be dubbed the "ram" position. Balance and leverage were the key variables in stand-up wrestling because each athlete looked for offensive opportunities while fending off the opposing fighter's attacks. Another engaging technique, the underhook (holding under the shoulder), is mentioned in the *Iliad*. From this position, the wrestlers were proficient at a variety of preliminary grips or setup maneuvers. Foot sweeps were a means of unbalancing the opponent in preparation for a strong throw. The waist lock was also popular and could be applied from the front or behind one's foe.

Many art renderings also illustrate finishing moves, such as the shoulder throw and the "heave." The latter was often

The "heave" was a finishing throw whereby the defeated wrestler was dropped on his head.

used as a counter to a leg-tackle takedown. The top fighter would sprawl his weight on top of his opponent, grasp him around the waist, hoist him feet first into the air and throw him to the ground on his head. A front choke was another possible counter to the takedown, but this was seen more in pankration matches.

The grappling techniques employed in the wrestling events had specialized names based on the part of the body to which a given hold was applied. For instance, strangleholds were called *anhin* or *apopnigmos*, throwing was called *rassein*, gripping the neck was called *trachelizein* and hooking the legs to trip an opponent was *ankyrizein*. Some of the more specialized and frequently used moves included the *mesolabe* (waist lock), whereby a grappler was first lifted to make it easier to throw him, and the *tour de hanches*, or classic hip throw.

Plutarch called wrestling the "most skillful and cunning of sports," and many proponents developed an assortment of efficient moves and holds. Counterholds were employed against attacking holds to defend against and neutralize the aggressor. Particular wrestling styles were devised in various cities, especially Thessaly, Sicily and Sparta. The Sicilians were crafty wrestlers and were reputed as being dishonorable in their matches. The Spartans, on the other hand, attempted to prevail with strength alone. The spectators at the games were all well-educated about the details of the sport and applauded the performance of a skilled wrestler. Kratinos, a boy from Aigeria in Achaia, was much admired at Olympia for his expertise, and he was granted the right to erect a statue of himself and that of his trainers in Atlis.

Famed wrestlers who won at Olympia and at other sacred games included the incomparable Milo and Timasitheos of Kroton; the Spartan Hipposthenes, who claimed six Olympic victories, and his son, Etoimokles, who won five; Amesinas of Barka, who used a bull as a sparring partner; the Elian Aristodemos, who never got caught in a waist lock; and Isidoros of Alexandria, who never suffered a fall.

BOXING

Greek boxing differed in many ways from its modern counterpart. There was no ring, in the sense of a roped-off area, and there were no timed rounds. The boxers fought until one of them withdrew by raising one or two fingers to admit defeat or fell to the ground unconscious. Sometimes they were allowed a break for a short period to regain their strength and wind. Clinching, however, was strictly forbidden; the hellanodikes would vigorously use his switch on a boxer who attempted such a tactic. Weight divisions were unknown, so the heavier athlete was always favored.

According to myth, Apollo was the creator of boxing, although the claim is also made for Herakles, Theseus and others. Apollo, however, remained the main patron of the sport and is said to have killed Phorbas, a boxer who invited travelers to Delphi to compete with him. Apollo inflicted the same fate on all challengers.

The most famous boxing match in ancient mythology was between Polydeukes and Amykos, the king of the Bebrykes, who lived on the Black Sea. The latter would challenge all visiting strangers to box with him, and he would kill them in the contest. King Amykos was a huge, heavily muscled man whose boxing gloves had steel spikes concealed in them. When the Argonauts came to Bebrykes, Polydeukes courageously accepted the king's challenge and was able to avoid his blows with agile maneuvers and evasions. Although it was a very tough fight, in the

Bronze statue of a seasoned boxer wearing oxeis himantes, his face disfigured from blows received in competition.

Boston Museum of Fine Arts

The boxer on the right submits by raising his index finger.

end, it was Polydeukes who proved too much for King Amykos. Instead of killing him, however, he made the defeated king promise to never harm those passing through his country.

The boxers wrapped *himantes* (thongs) around their hands to strengthen their wrists. Up until the fifth century B.C., the thongs were simple strips of fine ox leather called *meilichai* (soft) that were wrapped around the first knuckles, diagonally across the palm and back of the hand (leaving the thumb exposed) and tied around the wrist or higher up on the forearm. By the fourth century B.C., a glove made of ready-wound leather straps was introduced. These were called *oxeis himantes* (sharp thongs) and had the advantage of saving time over the prior design. The new model left the fingers open and were reinforced with straps of hard leather, with an inner layer of wool for the hand and a sleeve up the forearm. This type of glove was exclusively used by boxers in Greece until the end of the second century. Later, during the Roman era (approximately 200 B.C. to A.D. 500), boxers used hand gauntlets that were reinforced with iron and lead, called the *caestus*.

With each change in the himantes came relevant developments in the sport's techniques. During the time when the thongs were soft, boxing required more agility, accuracy, speed and flexibility. With the sharp thongs, offensive moves were restricted, the blows became harder and more focus was placed on defense. The pace of the contest was slower, owing to the bulky

Illustration by K. Iliakis

Left: Originally, himantes were straps of fine hide that were tied around the knuckles, wrists and forearms.
Middle: Oxeis himantes were reinforced with straps of hard leather.
Right: The caestus was used in brutal competition during the Roman era.

weight of the thongs, and the fighters relied more on brute strength than skill.

The rules of boxing were submitted for the approval of the Eleans by the boxer Onomastos of Smyrna, who won the event when it was first held at the 23rd Olympiad in 688 B.C. It forbade holds, groin attacks, the reinforcing of the thongs with extra layers of straps and the use of pigskin straps. The hellanodikes carefully examined the thongs before each contest to make sure they conformed to the rules. Injuries, however, were frequent and often fatal. Boxers who killed their opponents included Kleomedes of Astypalaia, who subsequently went mad, and Diognetos of Crete. Boxers were easily identified by their flattened noses and cauliflower ears.

It was not until the 48th Olympiad in 588 B.C. that a more technical form of boxing was introduced into the competition by Pythagoras of Samos. Sporting long hair and wearing purple, Pythagoras entered the boys' division only to be turned away for being too old. He then took part in the men's bouts and came away the winner. In contrast to Onomastos, Pythagoras' innovation manifested in the triumph of skill and strategy over brute force. Interestingly, this is similar to the story of Apollo, believed to be the mythical god of boxing, who defeated Ares, the god of war, in a boxing match in the initial Olympic festival. Here, too, skill prevailed over brutality.

Feinting and elusive footwork became more important than slugging it out toe-to-toe. The boxers closed in on one another on their toes, with small steps, shifting their weight from one knee to the other. Positioning was critical to the Greek boxer. Because the contests took place outdoors, having one's back to the sun was a major tactical advantage. For this reason, there was much movement by the fighters. In their ready stance, the left arm was extended and used as a guarding tool, although it was also used to strike. When combined with a lunge, it was capable of scoring a knockout. A two-fisted attack, however, was needed to win contests. The rear arm was the major offensive weapon and delivered a variety of powerful blows. These included straight punches, short uppercuts and hooks, and downward chops. The majority of the blows were directed to the head, although a concentrated assault on the body was also common. The ancient Greeks were among the first combat athletes to understand the effectiveness of body punching and observed the motto, "Kill the body and the head will die." The body was a larger and less mobile target than the head and could be assaulted repeatedly to wear down an opponent, setting him up for a knockout blow.

Ancient texts mention disfigured fighters whose eyes had been poked out by punches with an extended thumb, suggesting that blinding one's adversary was not a rarity. One vase painting indicates that groin strikes were also fair game. In some instances, a potent punch was all that was needed to secure a victory, as was the case with Glaukos of Karystos; he won his first Olympic outing with punching power alone, although he received numerous painful injuries against more skilled opponents in the process.

More so than other combat events, boxing was considered by the Greeks to be the most hazardous. An inscription from the first century B.C. begins by saying that "a boxer's victory is gained in blood." Kleitomachos of Thebes could attest to this when he was scheduled to compete in boxing and then pankration on the same day. Preferring the limb twisting and kicking of pankration to the relentless punches of boxing, he asked the officials to alter the

British Musuem, London

Boxers exchange straight punches to the head.

usual order of the events and hold the pankration contest first because emerging unscathed from a boxing match was virtually impossible. In the words of one Greek boxer, escaping defeat in a particularly brutal match was like "scorning death."

PANKRATION

Pankration, from the Greek words *pan* (all) and *krates* (powerful), was the earliest no-holds-barred combat sport. It could also be described as ancient mixed martial arts because the techniques were essentially a brutal combination of Greek boxing and wrestling. The rules permitted virtually anything, with the exception of biting and eye gouging. The groin was in no way off-limits to strikes and grabs. There were no rounds, weight classifications or formal ring areas; the action took place in the pit of an outdoor stadium. There was, however, an age distinction, with a boys' division added at the Pythian games in 346 B.C. and at the 145th Olympiad in 200 B.C. The competitors sometimes wore light boxing thongs to protect their hands. Victory was determined when a contestant either held up an index finger to signal defeat or was unable to continue. Fatalities were common. Being such a rugged event, pankration attracted only the fittest athletes, and those who competed had to possess great *kartereia* (toughness). Injury was unavoidable because competitors sought to win by all possible means, ignoring the danger to the bodies and even to the lives of their opponents.

The rules against biting and gouging were strictly enforced by the hellanodikes, who carried a stout rod or switch that was used at the slightest infraction, although sharp blows from the switch became preferable in the heat of battle to being maimed or defeated by a stronger opponent. Regardless, many who emerged from pankration contests, even the victors, did so with bite wounds and impaired vision. The philosopher Epiktetos noted that being gouged was one of the hazards of a career in pankration. (Incredibly, the Spartans and members of many of the Doric city-states competed in an even more brutal version of the sport that allowed biting and gouging.)

The terrain on which pankration contests took place was an area of dug-up, somewhat soft sand called a *skamma*. Because there were neither mats nor smooth, boxing-ring-style surfaces available during these times, the skamma limited rapid lateral moves, which made size and strength even more critical. The skamma also lent itself to motion with practical applications to the battlefield.

There were two forms of sport pankration: *ano* or *orthostadin* (upright) pankration and

Although eye gouging was a punishable offense in pankration contests, fighters often resorted to such tactics.

kato (down) pankration. Ano pankration, like modern kickboxing, required that both combatants remain standing. This was considered the safer version and was reserved for training or for early preliminary matches. Whereas striking was not allowed in wrestling and grappling was not allowed in boxing, kato pankration integrated both. When standing, the goal of the pankratiast was to land lethal blows in order to render the opponent either helpless or senseless. Once the fight went to the ground, the nature of the battle changed dramatically. Rolling on the sand or in the muddied skamma, the contestants grappled with the intent of submitting the other via a choke or joint lock. Strikes were also commonly employed on the ground to weaken the opposing combatant. There are numerous depictions of fighters in various top-mount positions, pummeling opponents with their fists.

Evidence shows that pankration was the most important of all athletic contests. At one tournament in the city of Aphrodisia in Asia Minor, the winner of the pankration event was awarded 3,000 dinarii (about $360,000), while the pentathlon victor earned only 500 dinarii (about $60,000). This sum was especially impressive because the tournaments at Aphrodisia were relatively small affairs.

PREPARING FOR COMPETITION

Much of the training of athletes was conducted in the palaistra and gymnasium. The palaistra was a private school that was established and operated by specialized trainers. The gymnasium, on the other hand, was a public facility supervised by a *gymnasiarchos,* who was responsible for its management. The gymnasia may have been initially designed for military training, and they were closely allied with religious rites; this is confirmed by their proximity to temples of worship in the cities. Evidence supplied by archaeological excavation and literary research places the first Athenian palaistrae and gymnasia in the sixth century B.C. The three oldest gymnasia were the Academy, the Lyceum and the Cynosarges.

Pankratiasts trained in a separate room of the gymnasium, known as the *korykeion,* which was guarded by a statue of Hermes, considered by many to be the mythical inventor of wrestling. The training was supervised by the *gymnastes,* who provided the diet and exercises, and by the *paidotribes,* who taught the technical skills. The paidotribes was usually a veteran athlete with an education in training methodology.

The city-states often funded trainers for the younger combat athletes because sport was an integral part of their military preparedness. Those who trained the competitors for any of the major festivals, however, were sometimes former champions and were paid substantial wages. They accompanied their students to the contests and served as their coaches during their matches. It was not uncommon for a wealthy patron to subsidize a promising fighter.

The gymnastes and paidotribes worked together to prepare the athlete for his particular sport. The gymnastes had a greater knowledge of training and outlined the specifics of the program, which was implemented by the paidotribes, who also followed the athlete's progress and provided support and guidance. The paidotribes was also responsible for teaching the holds and techniques of the sport. Many of the athletes who attained Olympic glory honored their gymnastes and paidotribes by erecting statues of them adjacent to their own.

The *aleiptes* (anointer) also was an important part of the team. His job was to oil the bodies of the athletes preparing to exercise. This developed into a scientific massaging of the

Illustration by K. Iliakis

Combat athletes practice the heavy events in an open-air gymnasium.

muscles, which became a great benefit to their physical well-being. It not only helped them limber up before working out but also assisted the process of winding down and recovering after long, demanding training sessions. Oiling was particularly beneficial to the pankratiast and wrestler because it helped keep the skin supple and reduce abrasions.

Each of the heavy events was an integral part of the school curriculum and was considered just as important to one's overall development as academics. Every male student was required to earn credits in various athletic endeavors. The Greek system of education integrated and related athletics, courage, honor and knowledge to a way of life. Boxing, wrestling and pankration were taught progressively as a kind of drill to either a pair of pupils or to an entire class arranged in pairs. After mastering the basic movements and their numerous combinations, students proceeded to "loose play," or free sparring.

The boxers used small punching bags for striking. The pankratiasts practiced their kicks and punches on a larger, heavier wineskin sack filled with sand or meal and hung at shoulder height, with its base a few inches from the floor. Both devices were used to develop punching combinations and kicking power. In addition, a swinging bag enabled the fighters to resist an opponent's momentum. Philostratos wrote that the pankratiast's punching bag "should also be used to maintain balance and to withstand the onslaught of its rebound. The shoulders and fingers are to be exercised against some resistance and all the upright positions of the pankration are to be assumed."

Wrestlers frequently plied their trade by learning various tactics with a cooperative partner who would follow and not resist. The bulk of their practice involved wrestling rigorously, while pankratiasts and especially boxers sparred lightly to avoid injury before a contest. This

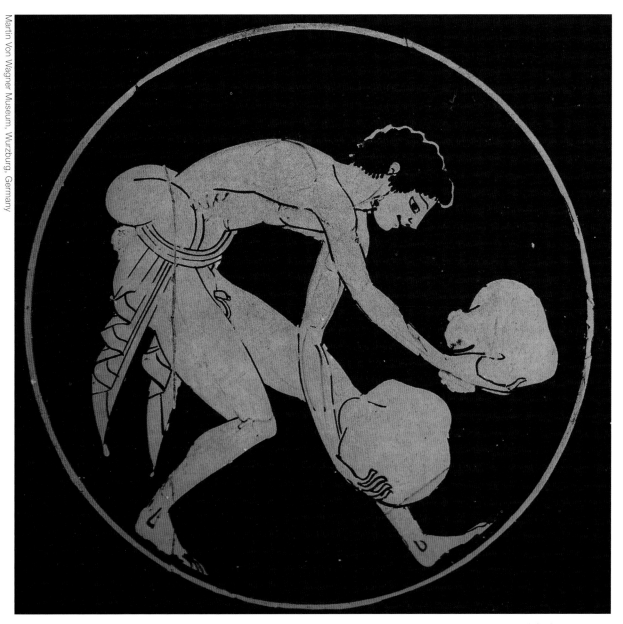

Weightlifting played an important role in the Greek combat athlete's training regimen. Stones were lifted to increase one's strength.

Martin Von Wagner Museum, Wurzburg, Germany

was called *akrocheirismos* (light sparring) and was conducted with padded gloves and special headgear. The headgear was also worn by boxers and consisted of two circular pieces of thick leather that covered the ears and fastened with thin straps over the head and under the jaw. Occasionally, they were made of metal.

Other training methods engaged in by those competing in the heavy events included weightlifting and *pyx atremizein*—a test of endurance in which the athlete stood motionless with his arms stretched out either in front or above. Many of the workout sessions attracted large crowds of spectators, and the combatants often practiced to the music of a flute in the background. Like soldiers and other athletes, the *polemikos* (combat athlete) was well aware of the importance of rhythm in training.

Besides conditioning exercises to build endurance and strength, the polemikos often drilled on techniques without an opponent. In *cheironomia* (shadowboxing), he practiced the movements of *pyxmachia* (boxing), while in *skiamachia* (shadow fighting), armed combat skills were stressed. Breathing exercises were also essential to competitors in the heavy events. Ancient Greek theories of breathing stem from the writings of Aristotle, who wrote, "The soul is air: Air moves and is cognizant. Air that we breathe gives us the soul, life and consciousness." The athletes inspired by Aristotle's notion concluded that air was *pneuma* (spirit), the vital force of all life.

The preparation for the games was a psychological as well as a physical trial. At Elis, every athlete followed a sound regimen of training and diet. During the course of their preparation, the officials of the games judged them on character, morale, strength, endurance, persever-

Combat athletes often practiced with the musical accompaniment of a flutist.

ance, skill and technique, and they chose those who seemed worthy to compete in the stadium of Olympia. It was also essential to present to the Panhellenic public highly trained athletes who would offer an outstanding spectacle.

THE PYRRICHIOS WAR DANCE

Related to the skiamachia was the *pyrrichios*, an ancient Greek war dance. At Athens and especially in Sparta, where the art of war was the major concern of its citizens, these combat-type dances served as military training for men and women. Before going off to battle, the Spartan youth were taught to perform dances with armor, bows and shields for inspiration. These preparatory exercises were considered to be so effective that Socrates remarked, "The best dancer was also the best warrior." The ancient Greeks believed the pyrrichios was a martial dance devised either by the Dioscuri (children of Zeus) or by the goddess Athena in celebration of her and her fellow Olympians' epic victory over the Giants. Ancient Greek writings, specifically by Aristophanes (445 B.C. to 375 B.C.), tell us that it was an armed military dance performed in rapid steps and accompanied by a lyre and/or a song performed by the dancers themselves or by others who did not actually participate. Some mythical accounts credit the Cretan hero Pyrrichos, son of Achilles, as the true originator of the pyrrichios dance, when he first performed it during the burial of Patroklos.

Many sources, however, argue that the dance was initially taught by Zeus' mother, Rhea, to the Curetes (inhabitants of Crete). When Rhea hid the infant Zeus in a cave to protect him from his father, she asked the Curetes to perform a war dance, shouting and striking their shields with their swords, to drown out the baby's crying. After Zeus overthrew his father, the Curetes became the priests in the new world, and their descendents continued these war dances as part of their religious ceremonies.

According to Plato, the pyrrichios dance was the most important among the war dances because it was given by the gods to mankind as a divine gift; only the gods were knowledgeable in rhythm and harmony. In Plato's dialogues, the *Laws* and the *Republic*, he eloquently expressed his belief in the virtues of dance. For him, one who could not dance was uneducated and unrefined, while an accomplished dancer was the epitome of the cultured man. He described the movements as resembling ballet, but with a variety of attack and defense maneuvers with weaponry. The dancers were lined up and armed, ready for battle, and they moved with rhythmic steps amid the noise created by the clanging weapons and loud shouting.

Plato also mentioned that the art of martial dance was not only studied by men but also by women:

> From myths of old which I have heard, I am convinced, and from present day accounts I know of, that there are, in the regions of Pontos, countless thousands of women, called *Savromatides*, who not only ride horses, but who also assume an obligatory role, equal to that of men, in training with bows and weapons.

Xenophon was an Athenian soldier and writer who also wrote about the pyrrychios dance.

After reaching the ancient city of Kotyora (present-day Ordu) in 400 B.C., he organized festivals to entertain his troops, who had passed through almost impossible mountain trails and suffered many hardships. Xenophon wrote the following:

> After they had made libations and sung the paean, two Thracians rose up and began a dance in full armor to the music of a flute, leaping high and lightly and using their sabers. Finally, one struck the other, as everyone thought, and the second man fell, in a rather skillful way. And the Paphlagonians set up a cry, while other Thracians carried off the fallen dancer, as though he were dead. In fact, he had not been hurt at all.

The Paphlagonians, as they looked on, thought it most strange that all the dancers were under arms. Thereupon the Mysian, seeing how astounded they were, persuaded one of the Arcadians who had a dancing girl to let him bring her in, after dressing her up in the finest way he could and giving her a light shield. And she danced the pyrrichios dance with grace. Then there was great applause, and the Paphlagonians asked whether women also fought by their side. And the Greeks replied that these women were precisely the ones who put the king to fight from his camp. Such was the end of that evening.

Xenophon's description leads one to believe that (a) the dance was performed with swords, (b) the Thracians, carrying armor and swords, danced to the accompaniment of a flute, (c) the pyrrichios dance was a Panhellenic dance, and (d) it was performed not only by men but also by women.

The pyrrichios dance was at one point so popular that competitions were held among teams of Athenians representing their tribes. Like the athletic contests, there were three individual events, each for the three age categories (boys, beardless and men). The prize for each event was a bull and 100 drachmas (about $5,600).

The Turks, too, claim to have created this war dance of the ancient Greeks. However, it was not until the 11th century—almost 2,000 years after Homer—that the Turks first appeared in Asia Minor. The Greek's social life and the entire culture had a profound effect on the life of the Turks, with whom they coexisted for centuries. It

The ancient pyrrichios war dance.

follows, then, that the Turks also learned the pyrrichios dance, which obviously had a lasting impression on them.

Another significant war dance is found in one of the myths involving Theseus. After defeating the Minotaur and escaping from the Labyrinth, Theseus went to Delos. There, while dedicating a statue of Aphrodite, he performed a dance consisting of serpentine movements that represented the circles of the Labyrinth—a dance that became known by the people of Delos as "the crane." In *The Trials of Theseus*, Plutarch offered this description:

> It was around the Keratona altar or, according to another version, around the altar of Aphrodite, on which the Daedalic image had been set, that Theseus and his companions danced the Crane, which consists of Labyrinth evolutions, trod with measured steps to the musical accompaniment of harps. The Delians still perform this dance, which Theseus introduced from Knossos. Daedalus had built Ariadne a dance floor there, marked with a maze pattern in white marble relief, copied from the Egyptian Labyrinth. When Theseus performed the Crane at Knossos, this was the first occasion in which men and women danced together. Old-fashioned people, especially sailors, keep up much the same dance tradition in many different cities of Greece and Asia Minor, and it is the foundation of the Troy games.

9. ACCOUNTS BY ANCIENT SOURCES

The following are translated passages from some of the most influential sources of antiquity. They describe the heavy events, including the training that was an important part of them.

ON WRESTLING

Once only Milo, the wrestler, came to the games (520 B.C.), and the promoter summoned him to be crowned immediately. But he slipped and fell on his back as he came up, and the crowd shouted that he should not be crowned since he fell down all by himself. Milo stood up in their midst and shouted back, "That was not the third fall, I fell once. Let someone throw me the other times."

- Anthologia Graeca (circa 520 B.C.)

Let us turn to the wrestlers. The proper wrestler should be rather taller than one who is precisely proportioned, but formed like those who are precisely proportioned, with a neck which is neither long nor set down into the shoulder. The latter is, to be sure, suitable, but it looks more deformed than athletic, just as among the statues of Herakles, the more pleasing and godlike are those which are noble and without short necks. The neck should, then, be upright like that of a horse which is beautiful and knows it, and the throat should come down to the collarbone on either side. The shoulders should be drawn together and the tops of the shoulders should stand up straight; this contributes size to the wrestler and a noble appearance and strength and greater wrestling ability. Such shoulders are good guards when the neck is bent and twisted by wrestling, for they give the head a firm base, which extends all the way from the arms. A well-marked arm is the following: broad veins begin from the neck, one on each side of the throat, and travel across the shoulders to descend into the hands, and are prominent on the upper arms and forearms. Those who have these veins close to the surface and more visible than usual derive no strength from them, and the veins themselves look ugly like varicose veins. Those who have veins that are deep and slightly swelling appear to have a delicate and distinct spirit in their arms. Such veins make the arms of an aging man grow younger, while in a young man they reveal potential and promise in wrestling.

The better chest is prominent and protruding, for the organs are situated in it as if in a stout and well-shaped room, and the organs are excellent, strong, healthy, and showing spirit at the appropriate time. But the moderately protruding chest is also beautiful, if it has been hardened with ridges all around, for it is strong and vigorous and, even though it is not the best for wrestling, it is better than the other kind of chest. I hold that hollow, sunken chests ought not be seen, much less be exercised, for they suffer from stomach cramps, poor organs, and short wind. The lower abdomen should be drawn in—this is a useless burden to the wrestler—and it should rest upon thighs, which are not hollow but well-rounded. Such thighs press together and are adequate for everything in wrestling, and pressed together they give pain rather than receive it.

- Philostratos (circa 230)

ON BOXING

Boxing was the discovery of the Lakedaimonians, and Polydeukes was the best at it, and for this reason the poets sang of him in this event. The ancient Lakedaimonians boxed for the following reason: They had no helmets, nor did they think it proper to their native land to fight in helmets. They felt that a shield, properly used, could serve in the place of a helmet. Therefore they practiced boxing in order to know how to ward off blows to the face, and they hardened their faces in order to be able to endure the blows that landed. After a time, however, they quit the boxing and the pankration as well, for these contests are decided by one opponent acknowledging defeat and this might give an excuse for her detractors to accuse Sparta of a lack of spirit.

The ancient boxing equipment was the following: the four fingers were bound up so that they extended beyond the strap sufficiently to allow the boxer to clench his fist. The strap continued to the forearm as a support for the wrist. Now the equipment has changed. They tan the hide of a fat ox and work it into the boxing himantes, which is sharp and protrudes from the hand, and the thumb is not bound up with the fingers in order to prevent additional wounds, and thus the whole hand does not fight. For this reason, they also prohibit pigskin himantes in the stadium because they believe them to cause painful and slow-healing wounds.

- Philostratos (circa 230)

Now the Argos escaped the Clashing Rocks and had come to the land of the Bebrykians, bearing the dear sons of the gods. There, the heroes converged from both sides of the ship, descended the gangplank, and left Jason's ship. While most gathered firewood and busied themselves with spreading their bedrolls, Castor and Polydeukes strayed from their comrades and marveled at the trees and flowers growing wild on the mountain. Soon they came upon a gigantic man with ears crushed from the rigors of boxing, his mighty chest and broad back bulged with flesh of iron. He was like a colossal statue of hammered metal. Polydeukes attempted friendly banter with the stranger, whose name was Amykos, only to be met with hostility and resentment. Amykos challenged Polydeukes to fight, to which he responded, "In boxing, or may we kick each other's legs too?"

As the Bebrykians gathered beneath the shady plane trees, Castor went and called the heroes from the Argos. The two combatants strengthened their hands with ox-hide straps and had wound the long himantes around their arms. They met in the middle of the gathering and breathed out mutual slaughter. At this point, there was jostling between them in their eagerness to see who would have the sunlight at his back. By quick skill, Polydeukes slipped by the huge man and the sun's ray struck Amykos full in the face. Then Amykos, enraged, rushed forward aiming his fist straight at the mark, but Polydeukes sidestepped and struck him on the point of the chin. Then, even more aroused, the giant battled wildly and, hunching over, he rushed heavily upon Polydeukes. The Bebrykians roared applause, while the heroes on the other side shouted words of encouragement to Polydeukes, for they feared that the huge fighter would press him into a corner and finish him. But Polydeukes, shifting his ground this way and that, striking now with his right, now with his left, cut Amykos up and checked his attack in spite of his great size. The giant came to a standstill, drunk with blows, and spat out red blood, while all the heroes cheered when they saw the gashes around his mouth and jaw, and as his face swelled, his eyes became narrower and narrower. Then Polydeukes continued to bewilder him by making feints from all directions, but when he saw that his opponent was utterly helpless, he drove his fist against his brow, smack above the nose and laid bare his forehead to the bone, and Amykos went down hard, stretched out on the layers of leaves.

But he got up again, and the fight became truly bitter; they dealt each other deadly blows from the hard himantes. But the giant kept throwing his punches at his opponent's chest and just below his neck, while Polydeukes kept on battering Amykos' face all over. The giant's flesh shrank as he sweated, and from a huge man he was fast becoming a small one, whereas Polydeukes displayed ever stouter limbs and a healthier color.

Then Amykos, hoping desperately for a knockout punch, seized Polydeukes' left hand in his own left hand and leaned sideways in his forward lunge and reached down to his right side to bring up a huge swing. Had the blow landed, he would have knocked out the Spartan prince, but Polydeukes ducked out of the way, and at the same time he hit Amykos beneath the left temple with a crisp right hand delivered straight from the shoulder; and blood spurted forth from Amykos' gaping temple. Immediately, with his now free left hand, he planted a punch on the giant's mouth, and the teeth rattled loose. With blows that thudded ever sharper and sharper, he battered the man's face until his cheeks were crushed in. Finally Amykos fell flat on the ground and, dazed, he raised his hand and gave up the fight since he was close to death. But Polydeukes, though he had won, did nothing brutal to his vanquished rival, but did make him swear to never again insult strangers.

- Theokritos (circa 275 B.C.)

The boxer should have a long hand and strong forearms and upper arms, broad shoulders, and a long neck. Thick wrists strike harder blows, thinner ones are flexible and strike more easily. He should have solid hips for support, since the thrust of striking out will unbalance him if his body is not set upon firm hips. I regard fat calves as worthless in every sport, and especially boxing. They are too slow for both offensive and defensive footwork. He should have a straight calf of proper proportion to his thigh, and his thighs should be set well apart from each other. The shape of the boxer is better for offense if his thighs do not come together. The best boxer has a small belly, for he is nimble and has good wind. On the other hand, a big belly will give some advantage to a boxer, for it will get in the way of the opponent who is striking for the face.

- Philostratos (circa 230)

ON PANKRATION

Now you have come to the Olympic Games and to the finest of the contests at Olympia. This is the pankration for men. Arrichion is being crowned, although he dies at the moment of his victory, and the hellanodikes is crowning him. He seems to have not only overpowered his opponent, but the Greeks in the audience as well. They are jumping up from their seats and shouting, some waving their hands, some leaping from the ground, and others are slapping one another on the back. His astonishing feat has left the spectators beside themselves. Who is so stolid as not to shriek aloud at this athlete? This present accomplishment surpasses his already great record of two previous victories at Olympia, for this one has cost his life, and he departs for the land of the blessed with the dust still on him. But do not think that this is accidental, for he planned his victory very cleverly.

- Philostratos (240)

Pankratiasts practice a dangerous brand of wrestling. They must endure black eyes which are unsafe for the wrestler, and learn holds by which one who has fallen can still win, and they must be skillful in various ways of strangulation. They bend ankles and twist arms and throw punches and jump on their opponents. All such practices are permitted in the pankration, except for biting and gouging. Indeed, the Lakedaimonians permit even this, I suppose because they are training for battle, but the Elean games prohibit biting and gouging, although they do allow strangling.

- Philostratos (240)

At Olympia, there is a statue of a Sikyonian man—a pankratiast named Sostratos. His nickname was Akrochersies (finger man), because he would grab his opponent by the fingers and bend them and not let go until his opponent surrendered. He won 12 victories at Isthmia and Nemea combined, three at Olympia, and two at Delphi. The 104th Olympiad (364 B.C.), at which Sostratos won his first victory, is not accredited by the Eleans, because the games were not held by them but by the Pisans and the Arkadians. Next to the statue of Sostratos is one of a wrestler in the men's category, Leontiskos from Messene on the Sicilian straits. He was crowned once at Delphi and twice at Olympia. It is said that his wrestling style was similar to that used by Sostratos in the pankration; that is, he did not know how to throw his opponents and thus beat them by bending their fingers.

- Pausanias (circa 170)

Now look there! That man picked up the other man by the legs and threw him to the ground, and then fell on top of him and will not let him up, but keeps pushing him into the mud. Now he has got his legs wrapped around his midsection and he is grabbing his throat with his forearm and strangling him, and his opponent is slapping him on the shoulder in order to signal, I guess, that he has had enough and doesn't want, poor fellow, to be choked completely.

Others, upright and covered with dust, are hitting and kicking each other. This one looks like he is going to spit out his teeth with his mouth so full of blood and sand. As you see, he got a belt on the jaw. And the official—I take him to be one of the officials from his purple cloak—does not separate them and stop the fight; rather, he incites them and cheers the man who landed the punch.

- Lucian, from Anacharsis 1-8 and 28-29 (circa 170)

The following is a detailed description of the klimakismos technique (rear choke with leg hooks):

And having thrown the man completely spread out in the dust, Aikos got on the middle of the opponent's back, sending his outstretched feet along the spread out stomach and binding together a bent bond around just above his knees. He pressed sole on sole and encircled the ankles to their outermost tips; and having quickly stretched himself over his opponent's back, and winding his hand over each other like a wreath, he cast a bond on the neck with his arm, having bent his fingers; he drenched the heaped-up sand with soaking wet sweat, cleaning off the running drops with dry sand, so that the entwined man might not slip through the knot of his hands while sending hot moisture down from his squeezed neck. And while he was being squeezed by the sharp palm, the heralds chosen as overseers of the games wandered over, so that the forearm with the yoked-together lifting strap would not kill him. For there was not at that time such a rule, which their descendants made later on, that when a man is overwhelmed by the strangled pain of necks being stretched by bonds he gives over the victory to his opponent with sensible silence, having tapped the winning man with a shameful hand.

- Nonnos, from Dionysiaca XXXVII 594-609 (circa 400 B.C.)

Having already grabbed Arrichion around the waist, the opponent had in mind killing him and rammed an arm against his throat, cutting off his breath, while with his legs fastened around Arrichion's groin, he pressed his feet against the back of both his knees. He got ahead of Arrichion with his stranglehold since the sleep of death was from that point creeping over his senses, but in relaxing his grip, he did not get past Arrichion's stratagem. For Arrichion kicked away his heel, which put his opponent's right side into an unfavorable position, since now the knee was dangling. Then Arrichion held his opponent, who was not really an opponent anymore, to his groin and leaning to his left he trapped the tip of his opponent's foot in the bend of his knee and pulled the ankle out of joint with the violence of his twist in the other direction.

- Pausanius, on the death of Arrichion (circa 170)

And as to the wrestling? Those who engage in the pankration, my boy, employ a wrestling that is hazardous; for they must meet blows on the face that are not safe for the wrestler, and must clinch in struggles that one can only win by pretending to fall, and they need skill that they may choke an adversary in different ways at different times, and the same contestants are both wrestling with the ankle and twisting the opponent's arm, to say nothing of dealing a blow or leaping upon an adversary; for all these things are permissible in the pankration— anything but biting and eye gouging. The Lacadaemonians, indeed, allow even these, because, I suppose, they are training themselves for battle, but the contests of the Eleans exclude them, though they do permit choking. Accordingly, the antagonist of Arrichion, having already clinched him around the middle, thought to kill him; already he had wound his forearm about the other's throat to shut off the breathing, while pressing his legs on the groin and winding his feet one inside each knee of his adversary, he forestalled Arrichion's resistance by choking him till the sleep of death thus induced began to creep over his senses. But in relaxing the tension of his legs he failed to forestall the scheme of Arrichion; for the latter kicked back with the sole of his right foot (as the result of which his right side was imperiled since now his knee was hanging unsupported), then with his groin he holds his adversary tight till he can no longer resist, and throwing his weight down toward the left while he locks the latter's foot tightly inside his own knee, by this violent outward thrust he wrenches the ankle from its socket. Arrichion's soul, though it makes him feeble as it leaves his body, yet gives him the strength to achieve that for which he strives.

- Philostratos, on the death of Arrichion (circa 240)

The pankratiast fighting for the victor's crown pushes away the punches coming at him with both hands and bends his neck this way and that, guarding against being struck. Often, he stands on tiptoe and draws himself up to his full height, then drawing himself back he forces the opponent to throw idle punches as if he were shadowboxing.

- Philostratos (Cher. 80-81) (circa 240)

ON COMBAT SPORT TRAINING

A *koryx* should be suspended for boxers, but even more for the those who are students of the pankration. The koryx for the boxers should be lightweight because the hands of the boxer are trained only for sparring, but the koryx used by pankratiasts should be heavier and larger, so that they can practice keeping their balance withstanding the onslaught of the koryx, and so that they can exercise their shoulders and fingers against some resistance. And his head should smash into it and the athlete should use it to assume all the upright positions of the pankration.

- Philostratos (circa 230)

If we were in charge of boxers or pankratiasts or competitors in similar athletics, would we send them straight into the contest without any prior training or practice? If we were boxers, for example, we would be spending the days before the bout in learning how to fight, and imitating the real thing as far as possible. Thus, we would wear the *sphairai*, in order to get the best possible practice in punching and counterpunching. If we happened to be short of sparring partners, do you think that the laughter of fools would stop us hanging up a lifeless effigy and practicing on it? Even if we were in a desert and had neither live nor lifeless sparring partner, would we not resort to a very literal shadowboxing, practicing on ourselves, as it were?

- Plato, Laws (circa 350 B.C.)

10. FUNCTIONAL ANALYSIS OF PANKRATION

Aristotle claimed that pankration's techniques were given form by Leukaros of Akarnania. Plato described it as a contest combining "imperfect wrestling with imperfect boxing," while Philostratos considered it the best and most manly event at Olympia. It possibly evolved out of the primative method of combat used by man when he came to grips with an enemy, be it another human or an animal.

Antikensammlungen, Munich

Thesi machis, the basic fighting stance of the classic pankratiast.

POSITION AND MOBILITY

In *thesi machis* (the ready stance) of the early pankratiast, the arms were held high and straight forward to guard the head and face, and the fingers were curled and open, ready to strike or grapple. The rear hand was chambered much higher and farther back than one might see in modern combat sports like Western boxing, *muay Thai* or mixed martial arts. The lead hand was also raised high to ward off head shots. The fighters aligned themselves using either the *systasis* (squared stance) or the *parathesis* (sideways stance), both of which were adopted from the sport of wrestling. The pankratiast could instantly defend against all striking techniques. The lead foot could be raised easily to shield against a kick while advancing or moving back, or to leap forward suddenly to deliver a powerful blow with the rear hand. Sources suggest that pankratiasts, like boxers, used nimble footwork and deceptive feints to set up their blows.

STRIKING TECHNIQUES

The strikes delivered in pankration were less damaging than those in boxing because pankratiasts rarely wore thongs on their hands. In pankration, however, the opposing fighter could be held with one hand and struck with the other, which was not allowed in boxing.

While boxing and ano pankration made use of a wide variety of hand techniques, such as hooks and uppercuts, the straight lunge punch was the prevalent strike in the kato competi-

Louvre Museum, Paris

The lunge punch was a powerful, straight blow to the chin.

tion. Numerous works of art reveal that most of the upright striking in the latter event was performed at long range. Once inside, taking the fight to the ground and grappling was emphasized over stand-up striking. The striking arsenal of the pankratiast was not limited to the closed fist. Vase paintings show the use of the elbow as a striking tool, and many depictions reveal fighters attacking with a multitude of hand techniques, including extended thumbs, extended fingers, downward hammer chops and backfists.

The hand strikes of pankration were no doubt influenced by the use of battlefield weaponry by the Greek hoplite soldier. The straight punch is similar to the thrusting of a spear or sword with an overhand grip, and the hammerfist is similar to the downward stab of a dagger.

KICKING TECHNIQUES

Kicking was also highly developed in pankration. In fact, it was essentially the characteristic that distinguished the sport from wrestling and boxing. Because the sport was an extension of battlefield combat, low kicks were found to be more practical and efficient. The favored technique was the front thrust kick, struck low with the heel to the knee, the intent of which was to break the opponent's leg. The same kick could also be aimed at the stomach or ribs. Some images suggest that this technique was more of a push-type kick, like that used in Thai boxing.

A sculpture on the Parthenon's wall depicts a fighter using the ball of his foot to kick a centaur, a mythical creature with a man's torso and a horse's body. The kicker's hand is used at the same time to block the centaur's downward blow, showing a high degree of technical skill and two strategies: a simultaneous kick and block with the hand, and the concept of "jamming" to close the gap.

Sweeping the legs out from under one's rival was frequently used, especially by the Athenians, as was clinching the neck and employing knee strikes to the body, head and groin. Although kicking was an essential means of attack, when the ancient pankratiasts applied this tactic, it seemed to usually be accompanied by a hand strike. Most of the kicking was of the front-kick variety, with no side kicks, roundhouse kicks or any

Louvre Museum, Paris

The low front thrust kick was a favored technique. Note the superb balance on the heel of the supporting foot and the low center of gravity, indicating a high level of scientific principles even at this early time in history.

British Museum, London

Parthenon wall sculpture.

of the more stylized techniques seen today in many karate and kung fu styles. There is no evidence of high kicks to the face or spectacular jumping or spinning kicks, which were likely considered useless in deadly combat by the Greeks.

GRAPPLING TECHNIQUES AND GROUND SKILLS

Whereas classic wrestlers controlled their opponent's upper body to facilitate a throw, pankratiasts grappled in a much more upright and balanced manner because a close-quarter strike was always possible. A number of throws and takedowns were available to take the fight to the ground; suplexes, shooting at the legs and clinching around the waist were all perfected by the ancient Greeks. Sometimes an opponent's ankle or foot was grasped while both fighters were upright, and the leg was lifted until the opponent lost his balance and fell backward. There are also many references to clinching as a prelude to ground fighting. Grabbing one's opponent around the waist or neck were common tactics employed by Greek wrestlers and pankratiasts.

There is a tendency to believe that pankration was essentially a striking art, even on the ground. But rather than focus on finishing holds, the objective of the pankratiast was to use grappling to take an opponent down, pin him and beat him into submission or unconsciousness from a dominant position (now called "ground and pound"). The first to fall to the ground was often in a precarious situation because his opponent could gain the top position and immobilize him with his legs, leaving his hands free to either strike or apply a chokehold. This pinning tactic was no doubt influenced by close-range battlefield combat, during which if a hoplite had fallen, he would be mounted and fatally stabbed by the enemy soldier. In essence, sport pankration was an attempt by the Greeks to simulate the style of movement and technical skills that the armored warrior used on the battlefield.

The kato component of pankration was characterized by submission fighting with joint locks and chokes—the dominant ploys to make the opponent quit. Many of these, however, were set up with hand strikes. Gaining control of the opponent through proper body mechanics dates back to pre-Christian times. Classic pankratiasts sought superior ground positioning at every opportunity. A coin from antiquity shows a fighter riding his opponent in a top-mount position while slipping his forearm under his throat in an effort to strangle him.

Among the favored submission grappling holds was the *klimakismos* (ladder grip), a move whereby the fighter sprang onto his opponent's back and applied a rear stranglehold while neutralizing his mobility by digging in his heels around the waist. The Eleans were particularly feared for their ability to quickly gain control of an opponent's back and punch mercilessly

Galleria degli Uffizi, Florence

A classic kato pankration scene. The top-mounted combatant applies an arm lock while preparing to unleash punches to the face and head.

Seizing the kicking leg of an opponent was one way of taking the fight to the ground.

to the face in order to set up a lethal choke. Another effective technique was the scissor hold around the waist, both standing and on the ground. It was used primarily with the ladder-grip technique because it left both hands free for choking one's foe. However, there is no mention of applying it when fighting from one's back. What has become popularly known as the "guard" is noticeably absent from any valid resource.

The *hyptiasmos* (back fall) was a key tactical move, popular among the slightly built contestants. The fallen fighter turned quickly on his back, using his arms and legs to protect himself. This was perfected by a Theban named Melissos, who executed it to win the event at the Isthmian games. Singing his praises, Pindar made an analogy of the tactic to that of a clever fox attempting to ward off a swooping eagle: "The athlete who falls to his back stretches out his arms in front of him and draws back his feet, kicking powerfully, just like the fox who, when the hook-clawed eagle rushes upon him, turns on his back to defend himself."

11. LEGENDARY GREEK COMBAT ATHLETES

LYGDAMIS OF SYRACUSE

t the 33rd Olympiad, Lygdamis of Syracuse became the first known victor in pankration. In a sport that was the domain of the larger, heavier athlete, Lygdamis' enormous frame was ideal.

THEAGENES OF THASOS

One of the most famous combat athletes of antiquity, Theagenes was the son of a priest named Timosthenes (though some believed his father was actually a god). Theagenes first came to prominence in the Greek world when he was only 9 years old, when he supposedly ripped a bronze statue of a god from its base and carried it home. The Thasians were so outraged by the act that they wanted him executed, but in the end, his punishment was to carry the statue back to its original place. The young Theagenes returned it, and word of his deed spread throughout Greece.

During the early part of the fifth century, Theagenes became an outstanding pankratiast and boxer who won 1,400 matches, the most of any Greek combat athlete. He won two Olympic crowns, one in boxing (480 B.C.) and one in pankration (476 B.C.), a double victory in both combat sports, and nine Nemean boxing titles. Theagenes also conquered athletes in non-combat events. When he traveled to Pythia, the home of Achilles, Theagenes decided to enter a running event called the *dolichos*, which he won. It had been his desire to gain a victory in a footrace in the homeland of the swiftest of heroes.

After his death, a statue of Theagenes was erected in Thasos. Pausanias related a story of a man who had competed against Theagenes but was never able to defeat him in combat. Each night, he would go and flog the statue, as if he were mercilessly beating the invincible athlete himself. On one occasion, the statue became loose from its base and fell on him, killing him instantly. The children of this dead man were upset by this and charged the statue with murder. The Thasians followed the law passed for the Athenians by Drakon, whereby murder was punished by exile, so the statue was taken and thrown into the sea. Thasos was then stricken with a severe drought and there was great suffering. The people sought the advice of Pythia, the oracle at Delphi, who told them to bring back all the exiles in an attempt to appease Demeter, the goddess of agriculture. After doing so, the drought and famine persisted, and the Thasians again had to send representatives to the wise Pythia. They were told that the gods were angry because they had forgotten Theagenes. Luckily, some fishermen caught the statue in their nets and brought it ashore to its original location, where the Thasians offered sacrifices to it. The drought ended, and the people of Thasos came to think of Theagenes as a god of healing.

POLYDAMOS OF SCOTTUSA

Polydamos came from the small city of Scottusa in Thessaly and was the tallest pankratiast on record. He won at the 93rd Olympiad in 408 B.C. Pausanias described Polydamos' statue in the Altis as follows: "The figure on the high pedestal is by Lysippos. He was the biggest and the tallest of all human beings except for the heroes as they are called, and whatever race of mortals may have existed before the heroic age. Of all the human beings of this age, this man, son of Nikias, was the biggest and the tallest."

Renowned for his great strength, Polydamos had a lifetime of endless feats and exploits that compared to those of Herakles and other legendary heroes. The deeds of Polydamos had never been previously accomplished by any mortal. According to Pausanias' narrative, in an attempt to rival the labors of Herakles, Polydamos killed an enormous lion on Mount Olympus without the use of a weapon. He also tore the hoof from a ferocious bull, and he brought a racing chariot to a complete stop with only one hand. He was most famous, however, for killing three of the Immortals, the king of Persia's royal bodyguards, as an exhibition of his skill. After hearing of his wondrous feats, Darius Ochus, who had seized power by tricking the Persian people, invited Polydamos to his court to make his acquaintance. When the great athlete arrived, Darius proposed a friendly match. Polydamos agreed and was attacked by three opponents, two of whom were armed with long Persian pikes and swords, while Polydamos wielded only a club. Within a matter of moments, all three met their death.

Polydamos died heroically in a mountain cave when the roof gave way. To save his friends, Polydamos supported the roof with his hands while his companions crawled to safety. Tragically, he never made it out alive.

ARRICHION OF PHIGALEIA

Arrichion had won two Olympic victories before the 54th Olympiad in 564 B.C. As noted in the book's introduction, it was there that the great champion's corpse was awarded the victory by the hellanodikai when he forced his opponent to submit to an ankle lock as he was strangled to death. In Phigaleia, there is still a statue of him in the marketplace.

THE ATHENIAN DIOXIPPUS

Dioxippus was an undefeated and feared champion who, in 336 B.C., accepted a challenge by one of Alexander the Great's warriors, Coragus. Alexander set the day for the battle, and it was attended by thousands of spectators. The Macedonians and Alexander cheered for Coragus, while the Greeks were behind Dioxippus. Both men were magnificent physical specimens, and each had a burning desire for the fight. All expected a veritable battle of the gods. The Macedonian resembled Ares, inspiring terror by his stature and the brilliance of his weaponry. Dioxippus resembled Herakles in his strength and athleticism.

As they closed in, Coragus hurled his javelin, but it was dodged. He charged with his spike, which Dioxippus splintered with his club. Coragus went to draw his sword, and Dioxippus trapped his hand and swept his feet from under him. As he fell to the ground, Dioxippus placed his foot on his neck and, holding his club in the air, looked to the crowd. This one-sided victory amazed the throngs of onlookers but angered the mighty general. However, Alexander and the Macedonians, envious of Dioxippus' areti, soon framed the pankratiast for theft and forced him to commit suicide.

CREUGAS AND DAMOXENUS

According to the writings of Pausanias, the two skilled pankratiasts Creugas and Damoxenus fought a marathon battle in Nemea around A.D. 170, which did not result in a decision. They agreed to *klimax*—each would strike a final, unresisted blow to the other. After weathering Creugas' punch to the head, Damoxenus instructed his adversary to raise his arm, exposing his side. He then instantly struck with a spearlike thrust to his ribs. The combination of his sharp fingernails and the blow's force drove his hand into Creugas' intestines, killing him on the spot. However, the judges disqualified Damoxenus on the grounds that he had broken the one-strike agreement by landing several blows (one for each of his fingers). The victory was awarded to the dead Creugas, and a statue of him was erected in Argos.

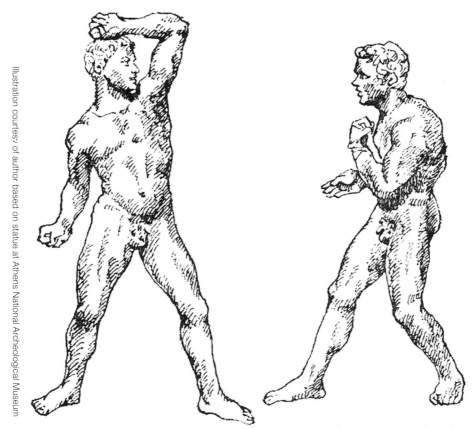

Illustration courtesy of author based on statue at Athens National Archeological Museum

Creugas and Damoxenus in their classic battle.

MILO OF KROTON

Milo was renowned as the greatest athlete from Kroton, and he is regarded by history as among the most famous wrestlers in the ancient world. He first won at Olympia in the boys' division in 540 B.C. and returned eight years later to win the first of five consecutive titles in men's wrestling. He also scored seven victories at the Pythian games, nine at the Nemean games and 10 at the Isthmian games, and he attained countless other crowns throughout the course of his career competing all over Greece.

A disciple of Pythagoras, Milo is said to have composed several treatises. While attending a Pythagorean symposium, the roof of the hall began to collapse, and it would have crushed all inside if not for Milo's quick reactions. He was able to support the structure's central pillar so that his friends, and finally he himself, could escape without harm.

Theodoros recounted another story of Milo's bravery. When the Sybarites declared war and threatened to destroy the small town of Kroton, Milo appeared in the town square, wearing a crown on his head and lion skin over his shoulders. Like Herakles, he brandished a club in his hands and called on his fellow countrymen to follow him to fight the enemy. Their resulting assault was so devastating that the Sybarites fled, leaving many dead behind them on the battlefield.

Milo's superhuman strength surpassed even the most fantastic of legends. He would stand on an iron disk covered with oil and make fools of those who accepted the challenge to knock him off it. He would tie a chord around his head and hold his breath until the veins in his head snapped the chord. Milo would hold out his hand with his fingers extended and challenge people to pull his little finger away from the others. No one, of course, was successful.

In spite of having the strength advantage over his opponents, Milo was defeated by his countryman, Timasitheos, at the 67th Olympiad in 512 B.C. Milo was almost 40, and his rival was a well-built and well-trained athlete 12 years younger. He was beaten not by strength but through an effective strategy of tiring him out. The contest lasted hours, and Milo finally succumbed after much suffering. When the youthful Timasitheos' name was announced as the winner, the crowd rushed into the stadium, lifted Milo on their shoulders and carried him in triumph. Even Timasitheos was among those cheering.

Milo's life was filled with glory, but he died a tragic death. In Kroton, he happened on a dried-up tree trunk in which wedges had been placed to split it open. As the story goes, Milo stuck his hands into the trunk, the wedges slipped and his hands were caught. That night, wolves discovered him and he was eaten. An enormous statue of Milo was carved in Atlas, and an epigram on its base reads, "This is the statue of Milo, best among the best, who conquered seven times at Olympia, without bending the knee."

DIAGORAS OF RHODES

And now, with the music of flute and lyre alike I have come to land with Diagoras, singing the sea-child of Aphrodite and bride of Helios, Rhodes, so that I may praise this straight-fighting, tremendous man who had himself crowned beside the Alpheus and near Castalia, as a recompense for his boxing.

-Pindar, Olympian 7

In the opinion of many historians, Diagoras stands out as the most outstanding of the ancient boxers. A man of great size and unusually good looks, he was admired for his footwork and statuesque stance. His fellow countrymen traced the great athlete's glorious career to the gods, and Hermes was thought to be his father. In fact, Diagoras came from a royal bloodline, his mortal father being the grandson of King Damagetos of Ialysos.

Diagoras' unparalleled record included wins at the 79th Olympiad in 464 B.C., two at Nemea, four at the Isthmian games, several in Rhodes and many in Athens, Argos, Lykaion, Aigina, Pellene, Plataia, Thebes and Megara. Known for his direct style, Diagoras was acclaimed as a fair fighter and was held in the highest esteem among his fans and followers. A man of dignity and modesty, he was bestowed with great honors and glory that he passed on to his descendants.

Diagoras lived to witness the Olympic victories of his oldest and second sons, Damagetos and Akousilaos. In 448 B.C. at the 83rd Olympiad, Damagetos won the second of his two victories for pankration, and Akousilaos was victorious in boxing. The sons carried their father on their shoulders while the adoring crowd showered them with flowers and laurel leaves. Suddenly, a Spartan's voice was heard among the cheering crowd, "Die now, Diagoras. There is nothing left for you but to ascend to Olympus to become a god." The joyous Diagoras heard the voice, and on the shoulders of his sons and in their embrace, he bent his head, wearing the two crowns, and died.

Although he would not ascend to Olympus, he would remain immortal. An enormous statue of him stood at the Altis, with Damagetos on one side and Akousilaos on the other. Close by was another statue erected of his youngest and most notable son, Dorieus, who had three victories in the Olympic Games, eight in the Isthmian, seven in the Nemean and one in the Pythian. All the victories were in pankration. Statues of his grandsons, Eukles and Peisirodos, followed.

MELANKOMAS THE KARIAN

Many noted boxers competed in the Panhellenic games, including the renowned Diagoras; Glaukos, believed to be the son of the sea deity, Glaukos of Anthedon; the young Moschos from Kolophon in Asia Minor; Kleitomachos of Thebes; Kleoxenos, an Olympic victor who was never injured; Pythagoras of Samos, who came to Olympia to compete in the boys' division but was ordered to fight against the men and defeated them all; Hippomachos of Eleia, who no opponent was able to get close enough to hit; and Tisandros of Naxos in Sicily, a four-time Olympic champion.

None, however, aroused admiration and praise more than Melankomas from Karia in Asia Minor. According to writer Dio Chrysostom, Melankomas scored many victories without ever injuring his opponent or being hurt himself. It was common for boxers to sport crooked noses, misshapen and flat ears, and faces full of scars left by old cuts. Thanks to the fighting tactics used by Melankomas in his bouts, he was unmarked and had a face, Chrysostom said, "as healthy as a runner." In some cases, he would compel his opponent to submit without ever landing or receiving a telling blow. It was his belief that to strike another, to injure or be injured, did not constitute bravery.

Melankomas won his first Olympic victory in the 206th games (A.D. 45) and compiled an undefeated record in most of the stadia in Greece. He was unrivaled in his sport, and his boxing style delighted the crowds. His movements were light, free and simple. He used his hands solely to defend against the blows from his adversary, and he continually changed position, thereby avoiding the more violent aspects of the contest. Most, if not all, of those he competed against would grow frustrated and lose their composure. The opposing boxer would eventually become so fatigued that he would admit defeat. Melankomas had phenomenal stamina and was known to fight for two days with his arms held out before him without ever altering their position. No doubt his success was due in large part to his rigorous training. He exercised and practiced his sport far more than the boxers he faced.

Unfortunately, Melankomas died at a young age. Always the eager competitor, even while lying on his deathbed, he asked a friend how many days remained of an athletic meet. He would not live to compete again. Melankomas brought a fresh new harmony and grace to what was otherwise considered a tough and bloody sport. By transforming it into a noble contest, his innovations made him a heroic athlete among the Greeks.

SOSTRATOS OF SIKYON

Sostratos was a highly successful pankration champion with 12 crowns at Nemea and Corinth, two at Delphi and three at Olympia. An ancient inscription states that he usually conquered his opponents without a fight. He was known as "Mr. Fingertips" because he would dislocate his opponent's fingers at the very start of a contest to gain the advantage.

MARCUS AURELIUS DEMETRIOS AND MARCUS AURELIUS ASCLEPIADES

Demetrios and Asclepiades were father and son *periodonikai* (circuit winners) in pankration with undefeated records in all four of the Panhellenic festivals in Italy, Greece and Asia. Asclepiades was so feared by some of his opponents in one tournament that, after observing his ferocity in the early rounds, they defaulted rather than compete against him.

DROMEUS OF MANTINEIA

Dromeus gained distinction by recording the first ever akoniti victory in pankration.

OTHER COMBAT ATHLETES OF NOTE

Many competitors achieved fame by winning victories in two and sometimes three of the heavy events in the same Olympiad. Kleitomachos of Thebes won three crowns in the Isthmian games for wrestling, boxing and pankration. Kleitomachos and Theagenes were the only two ever to win the boxing and pankration contests in the same Olympiad. An even more difficult feat, however, was to win both the wrestling and the pankration events in the same Olympiad. Apart from the demigod Herakles, who was the first to do this, it was achieved by seven others: Kapros of Elis, Aristomenes of Rhodes, Protophanes of Magnesia, Straton of Alexandria, Marion of Alexandria, Aristeus of Maiandria and Nikostratus of Cilicia.

Two other fighters who deserve mention are Kleomedes of Astypalaia and Diognetos of Crete. Both killed their opponents in competition and were punished but were nonetheless worshipped later as heroes. Pausanias informed us that at the Olympic festival in 492 B.C., Kleomedes fatally struck Ikkos of Epidauros and was convicted of foul play. He was denied the victory and penalized with a fine by the hellanodikes. Maddened with grief, Kleomedes returned to Astypalaia and forced the roof of a school to collapse. Many children were killed in the mishap, and the citizens of the town retaliated by stoning him. Kleomedes lived, however, and took refuge in the sanctuary of Athena, where he hid in a box with the lid closed over him. When it was finally opened, neither he nor his corpse was found. The oracle demanded that offerings be given to Kleomedes, "the last of heroes, and no longer mortal."

ACHILLES

Along with the athletes, the Greeks found certain warriors to be favored by the gods. Among these was Achilles, who was given unprecedented status in Homer's *Iliad*. The seventh son of the hero Peleus and the sea goddess Thetis, legend has it that Achilles was dipped into the sacred river Styx by his mother in an attempt to make him immortal. But either she was interrupted or forgot to immerse the baby's right heel, which left that spot vulnerable.

Thetis passed responsibility of the upbringing of Achilles to Cheiron, a very wise and clever centaur. Cheiron taught Achilles many skills, including the ability to run fast enough to catch any horse on foot. Achilles is portrayed in the *Iliad* as a glorious individualist, noble and aloof to the point of arrogance. Still a young man, he comes to the siege of Troy from his native Thessaly to head a contingent of troops, his *Myrmidons* (ants). Achilles is the consummate soldier, able to wield his sword and spear with incomparable precision and power while effortlessly eluding his ememies' blows.

At one point, Achilles allows his best friend Patroklus to lead the Myrmidons in battle. Wearing Achilles' armor, Patroklus is slain by the Trojan hero Hector, who mistakes him for Achilles. Achilles, after learning of his friend's death, becomes maddened with grief. He mercilessly kills Hector the following day and drags his body behind his chariot back to his camp. At the *Iliad*'s end, Achilles remains alive, but his death has been foretold; once inside Troy's walls, an arrow shot by the Trojan Prince Paris (and guided by Apollo) will strike him in his vulnerable heel, killing him.

To the Greek mind, Achilles embodies the ancient code of honor, having specifically chosen a brief and glorious life over one that was safe and obscure. He considers his choice in this passage from the *Iliad*:

> My goddess mother says that two possible destinies bear me toward the end of life. If I remain to fight at Troy, I lose my homecoming but my name will be eternal. Or, if I return to my dear home, I lose that glorious fame but a long life awaits me.

12. INFLUENCES OF SPARTA AND ROME

THE MIGHTY SPARTANS

Sparta was unique among Greek cities, with its program of patriotic indoctrination and full-time military service for males. Located in the region called Laconia in southeastern Peloponnese, Sparta preferred to hold its own local festivals and rarely competed in the four major games, especially in pankration. It is speculated that the Spartans feared losing to other Greek athletes in this most manly of competitions.

Spartan males were prepared from a young age for a soldiering life and were taught to obey orders and endure hardship without complaint. They were taken from their families at the age of 6 and by 20 had joined one of two teams whose goal was to instill spirit and rivalry through gang fights between them. Their learning was mainly physical, emphasizing combat sports and war games. They exercised naked and outdoors in all types of weather and were subjected to routine hazing and abuse. Scrutinized and judged by their elders, they grew up fearing disgrace more than death. At age 30, they became full citizens and could marry, but they continued to eat and train with their fellow soldiers.

Whippings were a ritual in a boy's training in Sparta. Grasping an iron bar secured horizontally between the bases of two trees, he was flogged with birch rods the size of a man's thumb until blood sprayed. The whipping was stopped only when the boy released the bar and "pitched" forward into the dirt. Some would not let go until they were beaten into unconsciousness, while others pitched because they could no longer tolerate the pain. There were also those special few who, rather than display weakness, were beaten to death by their drill instructors. These floggings were even used as a form of competition. At the yearly festival of Artemus, Spartan youths were pitted against each other to find out who could endure the pain and blood loss the longest. As opposed to any display of aesthetic skill or self-expression, this was merely a demonstration of submission to Spartan authority.

Although the ultimate objective of the Spartan education system was to produce perfect warriors, the young men were not confined to the harsh life of military existence. Their physical training developed a level of athleticism that resulted in crowns of victory from the very earliest Olympiads. Thucydides suggested that the Spartans were the first to introduce two innovations to the games and in training that became fundamental elements of Greek sport: the complete nudity of the competitors in the games and the covering of their bodies in oil.

The ancient Spartans practiced boxing as a war exercise. Because they did not use helmets in combat, boxing was seen as a method to harden their faces in order to effectively ward off blows. Because skill was secondary to valor, Sparta had no regular wrestling or pankration trainers, but when one was assigned, it was mandatory that he was knowledgeable in military tactics. Sparta managed to produce several Olympic wrestling standouts, but little is known about the foremost pankration competitors. The Spartans, for the most part, were reclusive and rarely permitted outsiders within their boundaries. Most modern knowledge of Sparta is derived from ancient Greek writers such as Herodotus, Aristotle and Plutarch, none of whom were of Spartan blood. What is known is that a high level of violence existed in their pankration contests, including the biting and gouging that was banned elsewhere in Greece. In one furious contest, an Athenian pankratiast by the name of Alkibiades, who had trained at Sparta, sank his teeth into an opponent to escape a neck hold. Scorned by his opponent for biting like a woman, he disagreed, claiming he did so "as a lion!"

The Spartans developed new, utilitarian events that were consistent with the rest of Hellas. Unlike the Eleans and other Greeks, they cultivated group combat contests. Teams would compete on a remote island and aggressively strike, bite and gouge one another with the goal of driving the vanquished into the water. They also were the only Greeks to encourage no-holds-barred matches. Because these contests were meant to simulate warfare conditions in which death was the expected outcome, no other Greeks were willing to participate.

These unrestrained pankration rules tactics reflected the grim discipline of Sparta. In time, they quit both boxing and pankration altogether, reasoning that these contests were decided by one competitor acknowledging defeat. This was unacceptable to the Spartans, who thought they might be accused by their detractors of lacking spirit, so Sparta forbade its citizens from competing abroad; they could accept one of their own losing in a contest of skill, like running, but not in a combat event.

Sparta was devoted to maintaining the bravest and most disciplined of all armies. Between 490 B.C. and 479 B.C., Sparta joined Athens in fighting the Persians in three key wars: Thermopylae, Plataea and Mycale. Each contributed to the demise of Persian power and the rise of Hellentistic influence on the Mediterranean. Eventually, however, the Spartans' reliance on traditional battle tactics left them vulnerable to new strategies that were developed by the Thebans and Macedonians. But from the pinnacle of Sparta's fame and glory at the Battle of Thermopylae (480 B.C.) to its fall (circa 370 B.C.), the Spartans could justifiably claim to have the best infantry in the Greek world. They built a warrior culture unsurpassed in courage and military prowess.

GLADIATORIAL BLOOD SPORTS OF ROME

During the Hellenistic and Roman periods, the athletic ideal that had its birth in the city-states and reached its pinnacle during the time of the Persian wars spread beyond the Greek world as a result of the conquests of Alexander the Great and the spread of the Hellenistic kingdom. Wherever Hellenism took root, traditional buildings used for exercise and training were erected both in the new cities and in the smaller, more isolated settlements. At the same time, new festivals, modeled after the four Panhellenic games, were introduced, along with smaller, local contests.

The period following Rome's conquest of Greece (circa 146 B.C.) proved to be a crucial test in keeping the games alive. There was an economic and social collapse owing to the constant warfare among the Greeks and to the ravaging of the Roman civil wars fought on Greek soil; most of the localized competitions were discontinued and the Panhellenic games fell into decay. Two factors lent themselves to preserving the sporting ideal, namely the great prestige of the Panhellenic games and the preservation of the gymnasium as an institution. When the Greeks were enslaved by the Romans, they used their limited autonomy to pursue their athletic interests.

The Roman attitude toward sports differed from that of the Greeks, in that Roman festivals were considered games and the Greek festivals were considered contests; whereas Romans organized games for public entertainment, Greeks did so for honorable competition. The Romans' disdain for Greek-style combat sport was rooted in pride. The Romans were, for much of their history, conservative, austere people who, like the Spartan Greeks, took special pride in their military prowess and considered losing in battle the ultimate disgrace. In short, for most Romans, defeat in an athletic contest was too much like being beaten in war.

Olympia underwent an athletic rebirth with the restoration of its buildings and an improvement in the organization of the games themselves. New athletic festivals were instituted in the Roman Empire that beared the same names as the Panhellenic games. For example, there were Pythian games at Phillippoupolis in Thrace, Nemean games at Aitna in Sicily, Olympic Games at Cyrene in North Africa and at Smyrna, and Isthmian games at Ankyra and Syracuse. The heavy events of the Greek world were included in the public games of Rome. These new games were more violent and lacked the religious themes of the ancient festivals. *Pancratium* (the Latin spelling of pankration) played a role in Rome's early interest in athletic competition, but it was considered too tame for the bloodthirsty spectators, who found caestus fighting more to their liking. Statues of maimed athletes from late antiquity attest to the carnage of these fierce and bloody bouts. The crowds became immersed in the Romans' preference for not only the heavy events but also the brutal and bloody battles between gladiators or between men and wild beasts. Ironically, the Romans found the Greek practice of competing in the nude decadent, and their athletes wore loincloths.

Museo Archeologico Nazionale, Naples, Italy

Capuan fighters were armed with the weighted and spiked caestus on their hands.

The Roman system of caestus fighting known as *Capuan* boxing was taught at Capua, which was among the empire's oldest and most famous schools. This deadly sport was characterized by the use of iron-spiked gauntlets on the fists, and kicks, wrestling throws and takedowns, chokes and joint locks were allowed. The Roman poet Statius (45-96) gave this report of a noteworthy boxing match between the aging veteran Capaneus and his youthful opponent Alcidamas:

> Now courage is needed. Use the terrible caestus in close fighting; next to using swords, this is the best way to test your bravery. They lift their arms, deadly as thunderbolts, watching one another. They spar, feeling each other out, just touching their gloves. Then Capaneus moves in and starts slugging, but Alcidamas holds him off, and the elder fighter only tires his arms and hurts his own chances. The young fellow, a smart fighter, parries, ducks, leans back and bends his head forward to avoid the swings. He turns the blows with his gloves and advances with his feet while keeping his head well back. Capaneus is stronger and has a terrific right, but young Alcidamas, feinting right and left, distracts him and then, getting his right hand above the older man, comes down from on top. He hits home on his forehead. The blood runs.

> Capaneus doesn't realize how badly he's hurt, but he hears the yelling of the crowd, and stopping to wipe the sweat off his face with the back of his glove, he sees the blood. Now he really gets angry and goes for the boy. His blows are wasted on the air; most only hit his opponent's gloves, and the boy stays away from him, running backward but hitting when he gets a chance.

> Capaneus chases him around the arena until both of them are too tired to move and they stand panting and facing each other. Then Capaneus makes a wide dash. Alcidamas dodges and hits him on the shoulder. Capaneus goes down! He falls on his head and tries to get up, but the boy fells him again. Suddenly, Capaneus jumps up and goes at the boy, flailing with both fists. The boy falls and Capaneus bends over him, hammering him on the head. The crowd pleads to save the poor kid as his skull is already cracked and Capaneus is going to beat his brains out.

> The attendants rush in and pull Capaneus off his victim. "You've won!" they tell him. Capaneus bellows, "Let me go! I'll smash his face in! I'll spoil that pretty fairy's good looks that make him so damn popular with the crowd." The attendants had to drag him out of the arena.

From about 264 B.C. until A.D. 326, hundreds of thousands of slaves, criminals, war captives, professional duelists and Christians were slaughtered in the cruel "games" held at the many arenas and amphitheaters throughout the Roman Empire. Although these spectacles were nothing more than mass murders, a class of professionally trained fighters known as gladiators emerged among the carnage and gore. They were selectively bred and purchased, housed in special barracks, fed special diets and received expert instruction in the war arts by highly skilled veterans. Each style of gladiator fighting had its own specialized weapons, training methods and teachers.

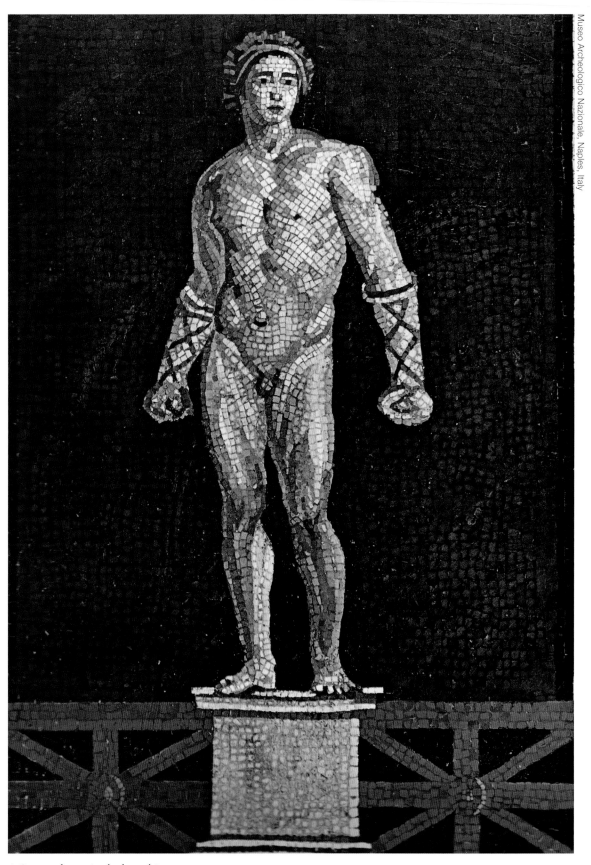

A Capuan boxer in the brutal Roman games.

Munera, meaning "offerings" or "obligations" to the dead, featured gladiatorial and wild animal fights. Along with other ideas and customs, the Romans borrowed gladiatorial combat from earlier Italian people, the Etruscans. The Etruscans believed that the death of an important figure required a blood sacrifice for his spirit to survive in the afterlife, and they staged rituals whereby warriors fought to the death outside of their tombs. The munera, along with other spectacles, also often celebrated the memory of important secular events, most notably military victories.

In Rome, munera were initially private affairs staged by aristocrats. Julius Caesar was the first leader to stage large-scale, public munera. Before Caesar's time, munera were put on by wealthy individuals who went to a *lanista*, a professional supplier of fighters, who procured and trained them. Caesar provided a bridge from the old system of training and managing gladiators to the one that prevailed throughout the empire, in which the gladiators were mostly prisoners, criminals, slaves who could win their freedom by competing or volunteers who entered the events because they offered generous prize money. Other gladiators were motivated by the physical challenge, the appeal of danger or the prospect of becoming popular idols who could have their pick of attractive and highly bred young women. A Roman writer of the period commented that the gladiators would pray for more fights in order to distinguish themselves and become more prosperous. Caesar, and later his adopted son Augustus, brought the munera to the general populace, who viewed the shows as entertainment rather than as funeral rituals.

The gladiators fought to the death. Pompey boasted of having 10,000 men killed over the course of eight shows. However, the combatants were not merely hopeless slaves condemned to die; they possessed special skills and were proud of them. There were *retiarius*, who used tridents and weighted nets; *secutors*, who used swords and shields; *dimachaeri*, who used daggers; Indian Sikhs, who used razor-sharp throwing rings; German javelin specialists; Parthian bowmen; Assyrians with their deadly, macelike flails; redheaded Irishmen armed with their skull-splitting, blunt shillelahs; and the no-nonsense discipline of the Greek hoplites, who used swords, spears or daggers.

There were several outcomes to these contests. If both warriors fought bravely and failed to beat the other, a draw was declared and they were allowed to leave the arena to fight another day. If the officials deemed that a contestant was not giving it his all or ran from his opponent, then he faced a whipping or branding with hot irons. Often, a gladiator went down, wounded, and was permitted to raise one finger in an appeal for mercy. His fate was decided by the official or the emperor, usually in accordance with the crowd's wishes. He would be spared if they pointed their thumbs downward and shouted, *"Mitte!"* (spare him), or he would face death if they pressed their thumbs toward their own chests (symbolizing a sword through the heart) and yelled, *"Iugula!"* (cut his throat). Another possible outcome was, of course, when a fighter killed his opponent. In some cases, a fallen combatant pretended to be dead, but few, if any, were successful at this ruse; men dressed like the Etruscan demon, Charun, ran into the arena and applied hot irons to the bodies. Any fakers exposed in this manner promptly had their throats cut. Male youths cleaned the bloodstains from the sand, and men dressed like the god Mercury (the transporter of the dead) removed the corpses in preparation for the next round of battles.

Gladiators were not the only popular attractions in the arena spectacles. There were also ferocious battles between animals, and between humans and animals, which were generally called *venationes* (hunts). While the upper class favored the armed contests, the Roman mob took a particular liking to the elaborate uses of man-eating lions, tigers and even bears. The execution of condemned prisoners by these wild animals was a particular hit and was a regular part of the events. At one show, Pompey sent out 20 crazed elephants, 600 lions and 400 leopards against men armed only with darts. Some hunters specialized in killing one kind of animal; the *taurarii*, much like modern matadors, faced bulls and attempted to stab them with lances. Stadiums were often flooded so that opposing fighters could battle to the death with hippos and crocodiles waiting to feast on those who fell into the water. Between the gladiatorial contests and the slaughter of animals, the Roman mob was always given a break with some form of more subdued entertainment. These intermissions consisted of dances, skits or trained animal exhibitions.

Up until the second century, there still remained some sense of fair play in the games. A gladiator had a chance to leave the arena alive. In this sense, the games could still be considered contests (albeit bloody, brutal and cruel) that gave the competitors a sporting chance, but they gradually degenerated into spectacles of pointless massacre. A popular display was to pit an unarmed man against one who was armed. Once the armed contestant killed his

Rome National Museum

Gladiators in combat with wild animals. The Roman leadership believed that the public should be accustomed to the sight of death.

opponent, he would be stripped of his weapon and another armed man would be sent out to kill him. This routine would continue all day.

Sadism became the order of the day in the Roman arenas. Claudius used to order a wounded gladiator's helmet removed so he could watch the man's expression as his throat was cut. Men were bound to rotting corpses and left to die. Christians soon became fresh meat in the stadiums, with some of the most horrific persecutions taking place under Marcus Aurelius in 166. Exhibitions of pure skill and courage no longer existed, and the games became a farce meant only to quench the mob's thirst for blood. The struggle between equally matched athletes had been lost, and in its place were acts of meaningless cruelty whose purpose was to satisfy the throngs of depraved and heartless onlookers. In spite of their disfavor, even the more intellectual Romans were helpless to prevent this lewd and deadly trend.

THE DEMISE OF COMBAT SPORT

From 267 to 361, there were no listings of Olympic victors. The preservation of the buildings and remodeling of the arenas during this time suggests the probable continuance of the games after a short interval. By the end of the fourth century, the games had fallen into the hands of unscrupulous promoters, and the spirit of competition had virtually disappeared. Rather than preserve the tradition of pankration and the other combat sports, these professional guilds did more harm than good. The athletic ideal that was born in the Greek gymnasia and in local festivals gave way to nothing more than a love of the spectacle, and monetary purses were the competitors' only reward and motivation. Cash advances were even offered to the more famous to compete in certain festivals. In the crumbling Roman Empire, the gladiator was finished as a highly trained professional. Obtaining wild beasts for the games had become almost impossible, and the Romans even ran out of Christians and criminals to publicly torture and murder.

With the increasing power of the Christian church, the games were finally abolished around 393 by an edict of the Christian Roman Emperor Theodosius I that prohibited all pagan festivals. This brought the end of combat competition (or what was left of it) throughout Rome. Lacking religious sanctioning, disassociated from its mythical roots and in the hands of professionals, athletics could no longer withstand the growing religious assault of Christianity. Competitions persisted in the Greek cities of the East, especially in Antiocheia, but the last of the games was abolished in 510.

13. PRESERVING THE GREEK LEGACY

With the abolishment of the games, many of Greece's combat sports saw their popularity slip away. Pankration, in particular, appears to have become a lost art in the years that followed. Fifteen centuries would elapse until the successful revival of the Olympic Games (in Athens in 1896), but pankration was not included as part of the new events.

THE REVIVAL OF THE OLYMPIC GAMES

The revival of the games sprang from two phenomena: the study of Greek literature and the excavation of ancient sites. When Greek scholars arrived as refugees in the West in the 14th and 15th centuries, conditions were ripe for European culture to embrace the Classical education of antiquity. Many turned passionately to the study of ancient Hellenic civilization, which led to the blossoming of art and literary works.

The first voice to express that man had the right to partake in exercise, games and recreation was that of Petro-Paulo Vergero, a professor and a prominent figure in gymnastics. The Olympic Games are referred to for the first time in the modern world in 1430 by Florentine poet Mateo Palmieri. The idea of resurrecting the Olympics was first put forth in 1793 by Guts Muts, the father of German gymnastics. In modern Greece, the ancient ideal of the Olympic spirit was not completely forgotten. In 1833, the newspaper *Helios* published a poem by Greek poet Alexander Sousos that illustrated the necessity of reviving the Olympic Games. It read:

> Plato,
>
> If our shadow could fly to your earth it would daringly shout to the Ministers of the Throne: Leave your petty politics and vain quarrels. Recall the past splendor of Greece. Tell me, where are your ancient centuries? Where are your Olympic Games? Your majestic celebrations and great theatres? Where are your sculptures and busts, where are your altars and temples?
>
> Every city, every wood and every temple was filled before with rows of silent marble statues. Foreign nations decorated your altars with offerings, gold jars from Gygas, silver plates and precious stones from Croesus. When the glorious Olympic festival opened, large crowds gathered to watch the games where athletes and kings came to compete, Ieron and Gelon and Philip and others. Before forty thousand bedazzled Greeks, Herodotus presented in his elegant history their recent triumphs. Thucudides listened to the beautiful harmony of his prose and prepared to meet him in competition as a worthy rival.

In 1838, when Greece won liberation from the Turks and founded the Greek Kingdom, the municipality of Letrinoi proposed that the Olympic Games take place on March 25, Greece's national day. According to their plans, the games would occur every four years. A wealthy Greek from Northern Greece, Evangelos Zappas, proposed a plan to the Greek government to cover all the expenses for the organization of the games. A.R. Rangaves, Greece's foreign minister, objected; in his opinion, the modern Olympiad should focus on agricultural and industrial progress, not on athletics. He proposed to Zappas a mixed organization that would include both agricultural/industrial competitions and sporting events.

The first Zappian Olympics were held in 1859. Because the renovation of the ancient stadium had not been completed, the games took place at Loudovicos' Square (today's Kotzia Square) in the center of Athens. Thousands attended, including the royal family and members of the government and military. The event marked the first mass gathering in the new era of the modern society. The industrial segment in the Zappian Olympics was held regularly and received more attention and far more monetary financing than the athletic competition, which was more gamelike than sportive. With the lack of genuine athletes at the time, the organizing committee accepted anyone attracted to the monetary purses of the games to participate. A newspaper article from that period tells of a policeman who was present to maintain crowd control and left his post to compete in the races, and of a beggar who also participated in the races. The first Zappian Olympics were the object of much criticism, but the ideals of the athletic competition were generally accepted, and the foundation was built for the new Olympics.

In 1870, the games were conducted again. They took place in the restored stadium and were better organized. The program and the rules of the games were published on time. Thirty-one athletes were chosen and each followed special, mandatory training. There were nine events, and the rewards were both monetary and symbolic. A band played an Olympic hymn that was specially composed for the occasion. The judges were university professors, and there was a herald for announcing the winners. This time, the games enjoyed immense success, and many articles were published praising them.

The third Olympiad took place in 1875 and was organized by Ioannis Phokianos, Greece's director of the public gymnasium. He strongly believed that gymnastics could be spread through the educated and cultured classes, primarily through high-school and university students who trained at the public gymnasium in Athens and used exercises taken from the German gymnastics system. In spite of the great preparation and even greater expectations, these games were not impressive. The royal family did not take part, and the large masses of people who attended overfilled the stadium's capacity, but there was much dissatisfaction. Phokianos, however, was able to achieve success in the fourth and final Zappian Olympics in 1889.

During this period, sport pankration was absent from the scheduled games. Some say the skills of the sport continued to be practiced in secret by pankratiasts who had concealed themselves in the many Greek mountains. Variations of the sport would emerge from time to time, with the various clans exchanging techniques and strategies in an effort to preserve their knowledge. In 1896, the only combat contest held at the games in Athens was Greco-Roman wrestling.

In 1898, an effort was initiated to resurrect pankration as a sporting event under the name *neo-pancratium*. R. Logan Browne, who served as the movement's primary promoter and spokesman, wrote at length for *Health and Strength Magazine*, describing the details of its restoration. Unfortunately, there is no evidence that he was successful in getting neo-pancratium off the ground. It is interesting to note, however, the similarities between Browne's vision of neo-pancratium and today's mixed martial arts, as described in these excerpts from one of his articles:

> It may be suggested that the pancratium is too terrible to serve any useful
> purpose in these modern times, save perhaps as a salutary reminder that even
> a society as civilized as that of classical Greece required an outlet for those

primitive and violent impulses, which, if left unexpressed within the confines of sport, might wreak havoc without. Vis-à-vis its unalloyed form, replete with the breaking of fingers and throttling, no gentleman could disagree. However, several years ago, it occurred to me that the ancient pancratium, suitably adapted, might afford us an excellent method of physical culture and athletic contest, with the additional benefit of being a secure and versatile method of self-defense against roughs and thugs.

In reconstructing pancratium for the modern age, our raison d'etre has been that whilst blows are legitimately outlawed in wrestling, they are the boxer's stock in trade, and whilst gripping and throwing are banned in the ring, they are practiced safely by wrestlers everywhere. By combining these two sports we may approximate the pankratiast's art in all but its most savage aspects, thereby enjoying its benefits without suffering its excesses. Our Committee has elected to name the result neo-pancratium, for although our experiments have referred to classical sources wherever possible, there are certain aspects of the ancient Greek practice that we have determined as being unsuitable for this more refined era. Nevertheless, we feel confident that this new sport will serve its several purposes most admirably.

At this point during our early experiments we found ourselves at the mercy of the same set of circumstances that plagued our Olympic forebears. Just as they discovered regarding the boxer's cestus, the modern glove, so crucial in cushioning the force of a blow, becomes an absolute handicap when wrestling. For a time we prevaricated, dividing our contests into separate bouts for boxing and wrestling, but this was found to be unsatisfactory. The solution has been to devise a novel form of glove, rather more open in the palm and with room for the fingers to grip securely, yet well-padded across the knuckles. This innovation allows neo-pankratiasts to successfully move between boxing and wrestling as required by the exigencies of any given contest. The Committee is presently undertaking discussions with a leading purveyor of sporting goods and hopes to be able to offer these new gloves to the public in the not-distant future.

The question remains as to how far we may follow our predecessors and yet remain within the bounds of civilized sportsmanship. For example, Englishmen regard pummeling a downed opponent to be the nadir of dishonorable behavior, and yet precisely this method was frequently the most successful tactic of the original pankratiasts in securing victory. Of course, in the extreme circumstance of a life-or-death struggle, the conventions of sportsmanship should not apply and one must do whatever is necessary to prevail, but how to translate this ethic into sporting competition? The answer has been, as needs must, to compromise by barring any blows against an obviously helpless athlete, who will in any case generally elect to surrender once it becomes obvious that, if he did not, more than his pride would suffer at the hands of his adversary.

Between 1923 and 1973, little documentation substantiates the existence of the ancient combat sports, especially pankration, either as a form of combat competition or as an art taught in Greece or anywhere else. Many historians believe that the original pankration vanished because it lacked the philosophy of a "true" martial art. To some, sport pankration was a futile attempt to bring battlefield-style combat into the Olympiad. But in the late 1960s, a new effort was initiated to revitalize the ancient Greek system of total fighting.

THE RECONSTRUCTION PROCESS

I grew up outside of Boston in a household where ethnic pride was everything, with a strong father who drilled into my head that one should be "proud to be Greek." I learned at an early age that to come home defeated at anything, especially in a fight, was unacceptable and—even worse—dishonorable. Perhaps this is what first fueled my fear of losing and my love of competition. Although I lacked size, I was coordinated and blessed with energy and drive, all of which would serve me well in achieving my goals later in my martial arts journey. Like others my age, I aspired to excel as an athlete. While most were drawn to baseball, football and basketball, however, I immersed my entire being into fighting. When I was supposed to be attending Greek school to better speak and comprehend the language, I could be found learning to box in a dingy, poorly lit gym. Boxing was my chosen sport, and I followed many professional bouts. Boxers like Muhammad Ali, Rocky Marciano and Marvin Hagler were among my heroes.

The "sweet science" equipped me with an undetectable lead, fluid combinations, and the ability to baffle an opponent with feints or by countering off a parry or slip. I also tended to favor mobility (standing there and trading leather was not my idea of good strategy). I knew firsthand from sparring what it felt like to be rocked by hard punches, so I spent countless hours perfecting my footwork and evasiveness, and I realized the importance of timing. As years passed, my learning was augmented by analyzing different champions and their attributes— Ali's elusive movement, Marciano's resilience and speed, Hagler's explosive power, etc. Once I became confident in my boxing skills, I began to serve as a sparring partner for those competing in amateur boxing shows and the New England Golden Gloves.

With a fire in my blood to compete, I achieved success in the ring, but an altercation with a wrestler taught me a valuable lesson: A good grappler can get underneath your punches and take you down. Once on the ground, it was a new environment because my boxing skills lost their capacity to inflict damage. I held my own in the fight, but I did not win. We had a good-size crowd on hand to watch, and I came away more embarrassed than injured.

It did not take me long to pursue wrestling at a local YMCA, and I practiced through high school and my early college years. Growing up in the tough streets of Boston and Lowell, Massachusetts, made knowing how to protect myself an absolute necessity, and my father totally supported me despite the fact that my chair in Greek school was frequently vacant. When I did attend, however, I carefully listened to my teachers, absorbing the myths and legends that shaped ancient Greece's glory.

Splitting my time between the boxing gym and wrestling classes, my confidence soared. Because I could count on getting into a street fight at the drop of a hat, being knowledgeable in both sports leveled the playing field against much bigger opponents. My trademark technique was fairly simple: ground and pound. I would land some punches to the face, forcing my opponent to raise his arms, then shoot low and tackle his legs. Once we were on the ground, I would straddle his chest and strike him in the face until he could no longer defend himself.

Although I continued boxing and wrestling throughout much of the 1960s, I also sought out karate and kung fu schools. After observing numerous classes, I never formally studied either. I found the kicks appealing, but the formality and rituals were a personal letdown; for me, horse stances, punching from the hip and practicing *kata* were all useless. Memorizing how an attack *might* occur was not realistic and was not of any value in preparing for a serious street conflict. Making contact while sparring, especially to the head and face, was frowned on, and I believed full-body contact was absolutely necessary to prove whether something worked. Traditional karate and kung fu teachers convinced their students that many of their techniques were so dangerous that they were capable of maiming or killing with a single blow. The problem was that most accepted this without question, which resulted in a false sense of security and even arrogance. I also failed to see any validity in wearing belts or bowing. Without question, I was a stubborn Greek who had his own opinions—opinions that were based on experience rather than on blindly accepting or conforming to untested theories.

When the boxing gym in Lowell closed its doors, I branched out into combat judo, where ground work and submissions were emphasized. There were no formalities or fixed forms, and little attention was paid to ranks. Again, I had no interest in attaining colorful belts; I wanted to learn the best techniques to use in a street fight. We came into class ready to slam one another to the mat, obtain a superior control position and apply a finishing hold to end the conflict. This training complemented my street tactics and wrestling perfectly, and many of the ground skills I learned would eventually make up the kato component of modern pankration.

Over the course of several years, I would log more than 100 fights, some more bloody than others, and I would meticulously describe them in my personal fight journal in order to later analyze the effectiveness of my moves and tactics, and those of my opponents. It became a game—my own specialized sport, if you will—one in which my life was always on the line. In one incident, I ended up on the ground underneath a much heavier foe who was drunk and in a wild rage. It happened so fast. We went down, and my hands were trapped as he attempted to smash his head into my face. It was impossible to hit him or reverse the position, so I resorted to what any Spartan would have done: I ripped off his ear with my teeth, got a hand free and gouged his eye out. I got on top and pounded him until he was unconscious. I learned that fighting is unpredictable and that one must do whatever it takes to survive. I vividly recall that remorse was not in my vocabulary.

Now in my late teens, I had become an avid reader of books on a diverse number of topics relating to combat. I had an impressive library, ranging from Greek mythology and Western boxing to an assortment of martial arts texts. I was particularly curious about lesser-known styles of both Western and Asian origins. French *savate*, Burmese *bando* and Thai boxing were just some that I explored, and I carefully dissected each one, searching for their best elements. My objective was to familiarize myself with as many different styles as possible and to "borrow" what I thought was effective. In so doing, I discovered the legacy of my ancestry, pankration, in resources devoted to the ancient Olympics. To my chagrin, however, pankration was defunct, and during my frequent trips to Greece, few of the native populace had any idea what I was talking about. The motherland had somehow lost its legacy.

It was my good fortune to meet Supachai Nitiayapatinai in 1967 while attending college. "Supercat," as his closest friends called him, was a foreign-exchange student studying in the States. He also happened to be a muay Thai champion whose uncle ran a school of top-notch fighters in Bangkok, Thailand. We quickly developed a great rapport and respect for each other, and we trained for hours every day, teaching one another our respective styles. When Supercat left the states for his homeland, I had the opportunity to visit Thailand and witnessed firsthand many of the best that the sport had to offer. Muay Thai opened my eyes to what a reality-based combat sport was truly about, but I thought that it, like many other martial arts, was incomplete when compared to what I knew of pankration because it included no ground tactics.

By 1971, my development had come full circle. I was content that I had evolved from a street fighter into what I believed was a creative artist. Certainly anyone can be a tough guy, but the best fighters have no need to act tough. At this point, I directed my efforts to accumulating everything I had learned and blending it together into one hybrid based on the concepts of the ancient Greek combat form. My mission was clear: recreate the ultimate fighting system of my forebears. This marked the onset of what I call my "research and restoration phase."

Rebuilding an ancient combat sport from ruins into an art form became a lifelong commitment. It required years of intensive research, rigorous training and trial-and-error experimentation. It is important to remember that, unlike today, few combat athletes were creating new styles bearing their personal preferences and ideologies, but in my case, I was not really inventing anything new but resurrecting something very old. A number of factors inspired me.

First and foremost was the lack of a comprehensive combat system. Stylized forms of karate and kung fu that dominated the scene in the '60s and early '70s were limited because they were basically oriented to stand-up striking methods and because none of them addressed ground fighting. Judo and wrestling, on the other hand, specialized in grappling techniques but forbade striking. A fighter was classified strictly as a striker or grappler, but neither designation implied that he was a complete fighter. At the time, cross-training in various disciplines was not the "in thing" to do, but it became a necessity in the development of modern pankration.

Ethnic pride was also a factor. The ancient Greeks' martial arts contributions had been overshadowed and almost ignored for many centuries. Although they were credited with influencing the Western sports of boxing and wrestling, the martial arts community was resistant to the notion that the Greeks, arguably through the conquests of Alexander the Great, laid the groundwork for the proliferation of martial arts throughout Asia.

Forming the nucleus of modern pankration's diverse tool kit were Western boxing and muay Thai's stand-up fighting, combined with wrestling and combat judo's ground combat. From this point, I studied anything that described the ancient art, ranging from its core techniques and training methods to its legendary stories on the battlefield and in the sporting events. For this, the analysis of friezes, artwork, vases and frescoes, together with the translated works of scholars and academics, were invaluable. Once the basic framework of my system was intact, all that was missing was a suitable name. Being Greek, it was pretty much fate that the word pankration would be the perfect fit. Whereas the native dialect expressed it as *pagratio*,

THE FIRST MIXED MARTIAL ART

the new version was anglicized as "pan-cray-shun." Its literal translation (all powers) and its roots expressed the essence of my MMA practice. The new name also underscored the fact that, although the modern system was built on the concepts of the original, it was a diluted form of the classic entity and was not handed down over generations, unaltered from its inception. As decades passed, Greek terminology was used to name many of pankration's core techniques, bringing even more distinction to the art.

To test my art without risking severe consequences, I considered my options. At the time, sport karate and full-contact kickboxing were popular, and no venue existed for reality-based MMA competition. It was not uncommon for me to walk into a dojo and put a beatdown on the instructor. I also found underground challenge matches for cash to my liking. In the years that followed, modern pankration continued to incorporate fresh, new concepts with the old. As the art grew from its infancy, scientific principles of efficient movement were added.

I opened the first modern palaistra around 1972 in Manchester, New Hampshire. Named Spartan Academy, the facility was located in a small office building and was fairly innocuous to passers-by because it had no sign and was not advertised in any way. Prospective students were carefully screened, and only the most promising and serious athletes were accepted. Training took place in strict anonymity, and I focused on quality instruction over student quantity. Particular emphasis was placed on the master/apprentice method of training, in which direct one-to-one teaching allowed the trainee to develop at his own personal rate of progress.

In 1973, I met a prominent martial arts journalist named Massad F. Ayoob. Intrigued by what I was doing, he decided to write an article on me and submit it to *Black Belt* magazine. At his urging, I ventured to Los Angeles to demonstrate pankration at *Black Belt*'s office. Although I was greeted warmly by the editor and staff, I knew I had to earn my place in their publication, especially because I was neither your typical stylized practitioner nor well-known at the time. After going a few rounds with some highly respected *karateka*, a month later I was on the cover of their November 1973 issue. This exposure to the martial arts world drew negative criticism from almost every direction. Many were unwilling to accept the fact that another art might have preceded the Asian styles.

I found that spreading my system during this time was no easy task because no organizations would sanction contests for my type of combat. The media became my gateway to promote my art, and I found plenty of interested journalists clamoring to submit articles on this controversial new subject. Although I was also teaching small groups of students in my palaistra and giving demonstrations at karate tournaments, I knew the exposure in magazines and on television would reach far more people and have a more lasting effect. This was, in my mind, the ultimate competition. Rather than only one opponent, I was solely taking on the masses in bringing recognition to Greece's legacy.

Throughout the 1980s, the palaistra in Manchester remained small but had a hard-core group of dedicated followers. Closed-door sessions were still enforced, with the bulk of the enrollees coming from boxing, wrestling and kickboxing backgrounds. There was also an influx of law-enforcement officers and military personnel during this time. Occasionally, traditional martial artists, from *kenpo* karate stylists to kung fu practitioners (many of whom were black belts), became students.

The 1990s brought dramatic changes to the academy, and training was opened to the public. Pankration had become more of a recognized name in the martial arts world because the reality-based revolution was taking hold. With the sudden popularity of the Ultimate Fighting Championship, many realized that pankration was the forerunner in no-holds-barred fighting events and the MMA movement. As a testament to its effectiveness, the palaistra trained an elite Army unit in the early 1990s in preparation for the ground offensive in the Desert Storm campaign during the Persian Gulf War.

The controversy surrounding pankration persisted, even as the MMA rage caught hold.

The November 1973 issue of Black Belt.

With the new technology of the Internet, a deluge of self-made experts bravely hid behind their computers and waged their meaningless debates. They hurled their biased opinions, but they essentially were clueless as to what modern pankration and Greek martial arts were truly about. In spite of this, however, pankration was reborn as a recognized form of the contemporary martial arts genre.

For me, this entire commitment to modern pankration dictated my life and became a mirror for self-realization. Being able to fight was only a part of the whole; the real essence of my philosophy paralleled ancient Greece's competitive ideal—to challenge and push myself mentally, physically and spiritually to the furthest extent. It was a means of tapping the unlimited potential within the human mind. Many live their entire lives without ever knowing what hidden talents they possess. I was fortunate to find mine early on, and it was my areti that provided the intensity and inner drive to relight the torch.

THE WORLD PANKRATION MOVEMENT

It was not until the mid-1990s, more than 25 years after the creation of modern pankration in the United States, that the sport found its way to Greece. Owing to the joint efforts of various martial artists, athletes and scholars, and with government backing, Greece's legacy had returned, albeit in limited form. For the most part, those orchestrating this movement were leading karate practitioners who had little experience in ground fighting. They were influenced by many factors.

The continued media coverage of pankration since 1973, the growing popularity of MMA contests and the upcoming 2004 Olympic Games in Athens finally alerted the Greeks to their martial arts legacy. Many Greek karate stylists, with their newfound sense of patriotism, did not hesitate to jump on the bandwagon. They even gave it a unique name, *pangration athlima* (contest of all-powers fighting). Greece established an international organization to help promote the sport. The Hellenic Pangration Athlima Federation, based in Athens, was formed in 1995 and solicited the support of representatives in the United States, Spain, Mexico, New Zealand, Iran, Russia, France, Australia and Canada. With a reported 200 trainers, 50 hellanodikai and a membership board of 15 directors, the organization's goal was to enter pankration in the 2004 Olympics as a full medal sport.

Because it was common for the host city to introduce a new event to the International Olympic Committee, there was optimism that pankration might find its way into the 2004 program. It was denied entry as a full medal sport, however. A second proposal was presented that designated sport pankration as a demonstration sport only, but this ploy was rejected in 2000 by the IOC. In the middle of all of this, the U.S. representative enlisted some well-known UFC competitors as coaches. Due in part to their notoriety and ground-fighting prowess, it was believed that their participation would bring authenticity to the movement. Seminars were held and promises made to those seeking Olympic glory. Most were unaware that pankration had already lost its bid for inclusion in the 2004 agenda.

There had been other problems, as well. Infighting was rampant among the Greek leadership, and the rules and format of the newly proposed sport were confusing and not reflective of true pankration. Originally, the new Olympic pankration was no more than a karate-based competition with limited contact. Because the majority of those running the show were karate stylists, they used this opportunity to get their discipline into the games. However, most who had read about pankration were not impressed; MMA fighters who were interested in competing remarked that it looked like "karate with some rolling around on the floor." When the IOC decision became known, many of the coaches discontinued their support. However, Greece did invite "pankration" groups to attend tournaments around the country. These turned out to be small affairs with the competitors dressed in traditional Japanese *gi*, with nothing to make it appear to be influenced by the ancient Greek concepts.

In parts of the world other than Greece, pankration more closely resembled its original form. Schools professing to teach the sport in Greece continued to be called dojo and looked like Asian facilities rather than Hellenic palaistra. In time, however, the Greeks continued to improve their rules and the action within the palaistra began to take shape. They permitted boxers and wrestlers to compete in their contests rather than show preference to karate stylists. The revival of pankration had truly begun making progress in the motherland.

In the United States, pankration instruction also showed signs of blossoming, but so-called pankration trainers only used the term as a convenient label for their amalgam of combat techniques without regard to observing and implementing Greek traditions. The tendency was to simply combine striking and grappling skills from muay Thai, boxing, Greco-Roman wrestling and either combat judo or Brazilian *jiu-jitsu*. (This had been my mission 30 years earlier.) To get around this, new names were invented for what these "pankratiasts" were practicing, such as American pankration, street pankration, etc. Some simply used the name of their school as a prefix. The problem was that, without the presence of Hellenic cultural features, pankration was no different from shootfighting or any other hybrid system.

PANKRATION TODAY

There appears to have been no term in Greek antiquity for "martial art" or even "technique." Today, Greek martial arts go by one of two terms: *polemikes tehni* (warrior arts) or *mahitiki tehni* (fighting art). Modern practitioners often use the term *mu tau* as a shortened form of the latter. (Mu tau is the English pronunciation of two Greek letters, *mee* and *teff*, which are equivalent to "m" and "t.") Mu tau consists of unarmed fighting methods, armed combat and the study of Hellenic traditions, history, myths and philosophy. Contained within this framework is a number of specialized principles and concepts. Without such an underlying base, pankration would be no more unique than any other form of mixed combat.

If we break down Greek martial arts in modern terms, they would consist of the following components:

• **Panmachia:** Total unarmed combat. This is further divided into sport pankration, which is designed for MMA competition, and Spartan pankration, which is geared toward street-based personal defense. Panmachia also includes the training methodologies needed to develop one's areti, technical skills and athletic attributes.

• **Hoplomachia:** The study of ancient weaponry, such as the kopis, *saunion* and dagger.

• **Hellenic Traditions:** The study of the mythical origins, history and philosophy of Panhellenic combat.

μτ

(μαχητικη τεχνη)

GREEK MARTIAL ART

PANMACHIA

Systemized methodology for unarmed combat.

HOPLOMACHIA

The study of ancient weapons for armed combat.

HELLENIC TRADITION

System of educational training fusing both modern and ancient traditions.

SPORT/STREET FIGHTING

Modern sport pankration and Spartan pankration.

SCIENTIFIC TRAINING

Aerobic and anaerobic fitness, bag work, ano and kato skills, drills, sparring.

MYTHOLOGY

Hellenic martial legends inspired by the gods.

HISTORY

Evolution of Greek martial arts spanning the past 2,500 years.

PHILOSOPHY

Hellenic combat concepts as they applied to sport and the battlefield.

In terms of physical techniques, modern pankration is an eclectic blend of tactics and moves extracted from other sources. It is very much like its predecessor, which combined the native skills of boxing and wrestling into a complete system. In this sense, modern pankration bears a strong resemblance to what is seen in limited-rules MMA competitions throughout the world today. At the same time, modern pankration has its own principles, history, philosophy, training methodology and core techniques that distinguish it from other fighting styles.

Some take issue with the fact that modern pankration techniques are modifications and not exact replications of the originals. No ancient Greek is alive today to precisely demonstrate the original techniques, and it should be clear that the modified techniques are necessary for applicability today; what might have worked thousands of years ago would often be inefficient now. In short, the goal was never precise duplication but rather modification and, above all else, functionality. Pankration's basic foundation is composed of the following characteristics:

Pragmatic Efficiency: There are no complex or flashy movements, flowery stances, or jumping or spinning kicks. In both its sport and hard-core street derivatives, pankration advocates functional, reliable techniques that require minimal effort and inflict maximum damage to one's opponent.

No Forms or Formalities: There are no traditional uniforms, ceremonial bowing, colored belts or preset kata. Modern pankration applies no-nonsense scientific attacks and defenses to end a serious conflict quickly and decisively.

Attack as Defense: Pankration is not a passive combat method that awaits the opponent's assault. The objective is to sense an oncoming threat of physical harm and react instantaneously. Although defenses are used to redirect and avoid oncoming assaults, they allow one to go on the offensive without hesitation.

Totality: One must be prepared to cope with any type of attack. He must be skilled in both upright and ground fighting, in striking and grappling, and he must be tactically ready to engage both single and multiple assailants.

Adaptability: Pankration training includes drills that simulate combat, so a partner is needed to test one's abilities in a noncooperative manner. Sparring with contact and protective gear is the best preparation because it conditions the body for impact and develops all the necessary mental and physical attributes for combat through experience. At the same time, one must be careful not to consider this activity to be the "ultimate reality" because it is done in a controlled environment.

Self-Evaluation: Special equipment is important in developing striking techniques because it provides better feedback than merely hitting air. Other than actually hitting someone, using various bags and pads that offer resistance and measure impact are the most precise means for evaluating one's striking skills.

Proper Body Mechanics: Brute strength is unnecessary to apply the skills of pankration. The key factors are kinesthetic awareness, quickness, leverage, timing, and above all, a calm mind.

Fluid Mobility: Unlike the static, rigid stances and movements of a classical karate stylist, a modern pankratiast moves fluidly like a boxer and must be capable of changing levels (i.e., go from standing to grappling). Constant motion creates a more difficult target to attack and makes one's offense more unpredictable.

Conditioning: Fitness is essential to executing the techniques with the utmost proficiency. Unlike many boxers and MMA competitors who train diligently only before an upcoming contest, a dedicated pankratiast makes training a daily regimen and a significant part of his life. Flexibility, cardiovascular health and strength are very important. To enhance flexibility, stretching exercises for the neck, lower back, waist and legs are included. Cardio fitness can be accomplished through aerobics, running, bicycling, jumping rope, running stairs and shadow-boxing. For strength training, free weights or any resistance apparatus are of optimal benefit.

According to Philostratos, the perfect pankratiasts of antiquity were those athletes whose physical builds were such that one might describe them as "the best wrestlers among the boxers and the best boxers among the wrestlers." Psychological qualities, such as courage and the will to win at all costs, were of equal importance. Pindar said of the pankratiast Melissos of Thebes:

> His courage in the contest is like that of the wild lions, and his cunning and craft like those of the fox. He does not have the build of Orion, and he does not take the eye, to look at, but in the contest he has unbeatable power. He is a man small of build, but with an indomitable spirit.

Does this imply that the modern combat athlete or MMA competitor who excels at striking and grappling and has superior athleticism and fitness is a true pankratiast? Certainly not. Although these qualities represent an important part of the whole, they do not constitute what a pankratiast is today. While one need not be of Greek lineage, he must possess knowledge of pankration's roots, its ancient traditions and cultural ideals, and have his own highly developed areti.

INSIDE THE MODERN PALAISTRA

The modern palaistra combines combat sport and self-defense training with a strong influence of Hellenic culture. Classic artwork, in the form of wall frescoes, paintings, vases and statues, dominate the decor. Ranging from mythological depictions and military gear to fight renderings, the art provides a feeling of being transported back in time to the gymnasiums of antiquity.

In addition to learning the technical skills of the system, students are taught the essential concepts that make pankration truly unique among martial arts; among the most pertinent are its mythical origins, the Spartan code of discipline, the terminology and the philosophy behind its effectiveness under any and all conditions. Today's palaistra must always remain true to the Greek tradition.

Training equipment also plays a vital role in today's palaistra. The equipment usually includes 6-foot-long heavy bags, double-end speed bags, focus mitts, striking shields, grappling dummies, mats and a wide assortment of protective gloves and head guards. The gloves rep-

Students practice a ground-and-pound drill at Spartan Academy in Boston.

resented perhaps the greatest obstacle in permitting total, unrestricted sparring in the early days of pankration's rebirth. Sixteen-ounce boxing gloves worked fine for stand-up fighting and even for takedowns and throws, [but we needed gloves that would enable one to strike without injuring his knuckles and, at the same time, allow the application of different grappling holds.] *Kempo* gloves were the initial choice, but it was clear that we needed a sleeker, open-finger design to better facilitate submission grappling. After testing several prototypes, we finally decided on gloves that closely resemble those worn by competitors in most MMA events today.

MODERN PANKRATION RANKS

Belts are not worn in the modern pankration system. The use of colored belts to signify rank is a traditional Asian custom and not of Greek design. Student ranks are indicated by lowercase Greek letters and instructor ranks by uppercase Greek letters. Written and physical tests are administered for promotions from one level to the next, all the way to senior instructor. The following *taxis* (grade levels) are recognized:

Mathitis (Student) *Taxis*
- *Ahareos* (Learner) Letter grade: alpha (a), beta (b), gamma (g)
- *Polimistes* (Warrior/Competing Fighter) Letter grade: delta (d), epsilon (e)

Paidotribes (Trainer) *Taxis*
- *Voethos* (Apprentice Instructor) Letter grade: Zeta (Z)
- *Daskalos* (Full Instructor) Letter grade: Eta (H)
- *Deethaktor* (Senior Instructor) Letter grade: Iota (I)
- *Arhegos* (Master Trainer) Letter Grade: Kappa (K)
- *Kirios* (Grandmaster) Letter grade: Lambda (L)

ENDYMA

The *endyma* (uniform) generally represents one's particular system. In pankration, there are no traditional gi-type outfits, as seen in a traditional Asian dojo or *kwoon*. In the Spartan Academy, for example, the trainers wear what is called the *hitona*, while students train in a T-shirt bearing the school logo and either loose-fitting pants or trunks, on which the *meandros* (the Greek symbol of eternity) is a staple design. Often referred to as the "Greek key," the pattern stems from mythology and represents the endless winding course of the river Meander. Students also have the option of wearing wrestling or running shoes, although most practice without footwear.

The meandros pattern (the "Greek key").

SALUTATION (HERETEESMOS)

Modern pankratiasts show respect by greeting one another with the *hereteesmos*, or Spartan warrior salutation. Although its exact origin is uncertain, many believe that it was first used during the early Hellenistic period by the Macedonian armies under Alexander the Great. Others argue that it was introduced sometime later by the Roman legions.

The salute is an important aspect of Greek tradition. It is comparable to touching gloves before a boxing match. Before and after a training session, the trainer performs hereteesmos to the students and the students respond in kind. Before sparring, training partners exchange the tradition. This is also the case before any pankration contest. Competitors must salute to both their opponent and to the hellenodikes to permit commencement of action.

As class begins, students perform hereteesmos to paidotribes Nick Hines.

Photo courtesy of Jim Arvanitis

The hereteesmos is performed as follows:

The pankratiast stands with his feet shoulder-width apart and with his arms relaxed and hanging to the sides.

The palm side of the closed right fist covers the heart.

The fist is swung outward to the right, with the palm facing the object of the salutation. The left arm remains motionless at his side.

This motion is symbolic of areti. The practitioner is paying respect to the person being saluted and reaffirming his vow as a po-lemikos. The phrase *dinami kai areti* (strength and honor) is stated. This is the pledge of the Grecian combat athlete to always perform at the highest level, in accordance with the code of areti.

SYMBOLS

General Logo

The official logo for Greek martial arts (mu tau) is triangular with two classic pankratiasts locked in ground combat. Note the meandros around the border.

Palaistra Logo

The upper body of the Spartan hoplite is the official logo for Spartan Academy, the first palaistra to teach modern pankration in the 20th century.

Fist of Pankration

This represents the essence of Greece's martial arts legacy. It consists of three distinct parts:

• The cotinus (olive branch), which is symbolic of the competitive spirit.

• The classic architectural columns, which symbolize ancient Greek traditions.

• The fist as a tree rooting up from the earth, which symbolizes pankration's reigns as the oldest of all martial disciplines.

14. MODERN PANKRATION TECHNIQUES

For the first couple centuries since its inception, pankration was essentially a stand-up contest because of the early influence of pammachon. By the close of the Classical Period, the *paidotribes* (trainer) was careful that his students were more balanced technicians, favoring neither striking or grappling. A limited number of tools were practiced at each range in training so that fighters would be equally proficient at both. In the kicking range, pankratiasts favored no more than two kicks, and they were always aimed below the waist. The striking range emphasized straight-line punching. At grappling range, many of the clinches, takedowns and throws of wrestling were included to bring the contest to the ground where the outcomes were often decided.

The continued evolution of pankration produced athletes who specialized as strikers or grapplers. As to which offense was superior, the following example might give some indication. In the Olympiad of 212 B.C., Kapros, who was proficient in all three combat sports, won the wrestling competition earlier in the day. He went on to face Kleitomachos, who would later win the boxing championship, in the pankration event. Although both were excellent fighters, it was Kapros, the wrestling specialist, who proved to be the better man. Of course, many factors have to be taken into consideration before reaching such a conclusion. Given the diversity of skills, even the best MMA athlete can be defeated on any given day as we have seen time and time again.

In mixed-martial arts today, a competitor cannot afford to be one-dimensional but needs to be versatile in every phase of the game. Rather than favoring this over that, the main strategy in modern pankration is to gain a "skills advantage" over one's opposition and avoid his strengths while exploiting his weaknesses (i.e. striking the grappler, grapple the striker). Knowing what tool to use at which range is also crucial to the combat athlete's success in defeating his adversary and securing victory.

Although it is likely that many contests go to the ground at some point, they all commence while standing up. Whereas the upright component of modern pankration consists of footwork, striking, parries and evasions, clinching, throws and takedowns, the ground conflict differs dramatically and is more complex. One must be adept in obtaining a dominant position on top from which to render his foe either senseless from strikes or force him to submit from a joint lock or choke. He must also be capable of defending and attacking from his back and reversing a position of neutrality to one of control. Knowing how to apply leverage is paramount on the ground.

The following is a random sampling of the seemingly countless applications of pankration skills, divided into ano and kato techniques. The ano sequences are further divided into attacks from free movement and inside the clinch. The kato sequences are broken down into top-control attacks, tactics from the bottom position, waist-scissor counters, and countering blocked submission attempts (chaining).

ANO (STAND-UP) TECHNIQUES
FREE-MOVEMENT SKILLS

CLOSING THE GAP

Face your opponent in a left lead stance (thesi machis).

Take the offensive by landing a back-leg round kick to the inner thigh of his right leg.

Push forward, take your opponent to the ground and pummel him with punches.

If your opponent tries to avoid the blows by rolling onto his stomach, help him flip over and take his back.

With your opponent nudged off-balance, move in and clinch him around the waist.

Hook his left leg behind the knee with your right foot.

Force a tapout with a rear choke.

COUNTERING A KICK

You and your opponent face each other in a right lead stances.

As your opponent delivers a round kick to the body, use your right shin to block it.

Maintain hold of his leg and rotate quickly to your right, taking him down.

Maintaining control of his left leg, continue moving clockwise and step over it with your left foot.

3

Quickly step in and scoop the attacking leg with your right hand.

4

Grip your foe at the hip while stepping around his right leg with your left leg.

7

Fall back and wrap both legs around your opponent's left knee.

8

Straighten the trapped leg and apply a kneebar to submit him.

119

COUNTER TO ONE-TWO PUNCH

You and your opponent square off in right lead positions.

As your opponent attacks with a lead jab, you hit him in the face with a jab of your own.

Grip both legs behind his thighs.

Drop your opponent to his back and mount his chest.

As he delivers a left cross, change levels and shoot. By transmitting power behind his punch, your opponent's center of balance will be slightly forward and his legs vulnerable.

Deliver a barrage of elbow strikes to the face.

SEIZED KICK COUNTER

You and your opponent face each other in opposite stances.

Spotting an opening, you deliver a lead front kick, which he traps.

Push his head to the side with your left hand while gripping his right arm with your right hand. Use your left foot to push off against his hip creating space and preventing him from mounting you.

Swing your left leg across the far side of his head. Trap his right arm using both hands.

Hop in with your left foot as he moves in to sweep.

Allow him to take you to the ground.

Force him onto his back with your legs. Lock his elbow into your crotch and raise your hips for a side armbar.

ELBOW STRIKE COUNTER

You face your opponent at medium range with your right foot forward.

As he lunges and throws a right elbow strike, step in with your left foot while slipping your left hand inside his arm and hook his neck.

Clinching your opponent around the neck, go for the knockout by unloading a relentless attack of knees to his ribs and jaw.

Pull him forward and deliver a right elbow strike of your own.

Hook your right hand over your left hand behind his neck.

SHOOT COUNTER: DOUBLE UNDERHOOKS TO STRIKES TO CHOKE

Square off with opposite leads.

Your opponent closes in and shoots low for a leg takedown.

With your opponent's shoulders locked, land hard knees to the exposed ribs.

Change your grip by wrapping your left forearm under his windpipe.

Before he can make contact, slip both of your arms under his armpits and clasp both hands behind his back.

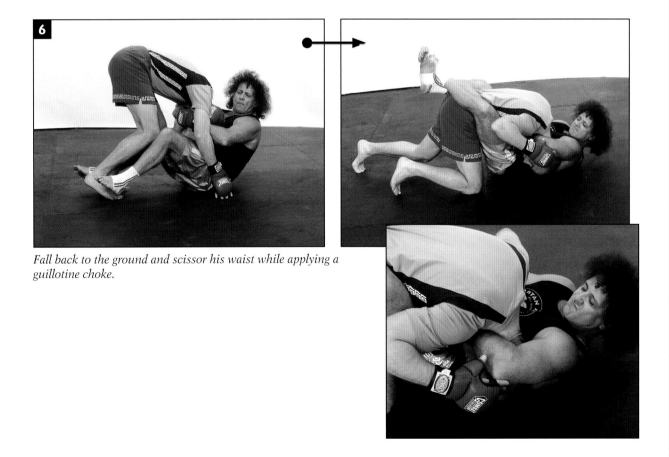

Fall back to the ground and scissor his waist while applying a guillotine choke.

SHOOT COUNTER:
SPRAWL TO STRIKES TO REVERSE ARMBAR

You face your opponent in a right lead stance.

As he shoots for a takedown, change levels.

Deliver a right knee to his head.

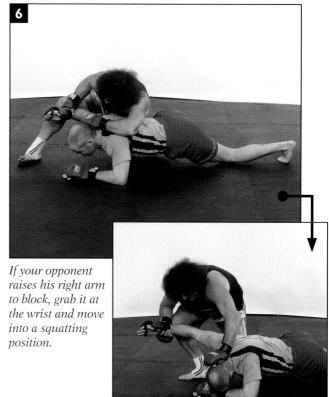

If your opponent raises his right arm to block, grab it at the wrist and move into a squatting position.

3

Sprawl by kicking both legs back and dropping your upper-body weight on his back.

4

Quickly move to your left into side control and pull your right leg back.

7

Turn to your right, stepping over the arm with your left foot, and pin the elbow.

8

Apply a reverse armbar by dropping to your knees. Lift up on the wrist, forcing pressure against the elbow joint.

SHOOT COUNTER:
KNEE STRIKE TO GROUND AND POUND TO BACK BREAKER

You face your opponent in a right lead stance.

Your foe shoots for a leg takedown.

If he tries to defend by scissoring you between his legs, punch him relentlessly in the face with both hands.

3

As he changes levels to be in line with your lower body,
deliver a right knee strike to his jaw. If timed right,
the blow will stagger your foe and send him backward
or knock him out owing to the force of his forward
momentum.

4

Once he appears hurt and
falls to the ground, move
in to finish him.

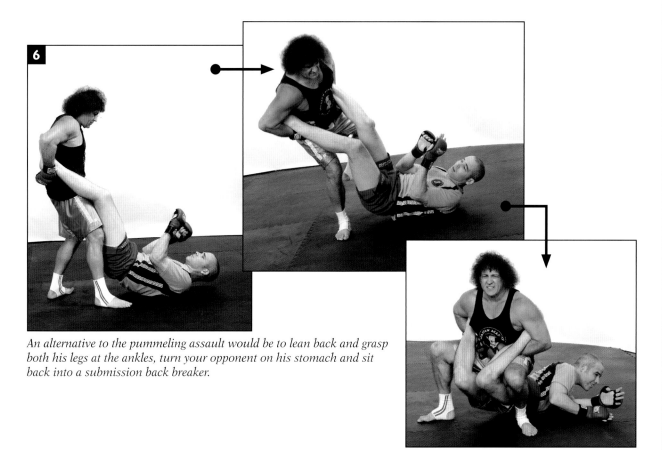

6

An alternative to the pummeling assault would be to lean back and grasp
both his legs at the ankles, turn your opponent on his stomach and sit
back into a submission back breaker.

SHOOT COUNTER: EVADE AND STRIKE

You and your opponent face off.

He takes the offensive with a high jab, which you evade by stepping back.

Free your right leg by stepping around and back to the left.

With your opponent on his knee, deliver a front kick to the ribs.

3

He follows with a takedown attempt, shooting deep enough to grab your right leg. Prevent him from taking you down by posting both hands against him.

4

Release your right hand and hook him to the jaw, forcing him to loosen his grip on your leg.

7

Follow with a hard knee to the body.

SHOOT FEINT TO STRIKES

You and your opponent face off at medium range.

As you shoot for the legs, he stops you by placing both hands on your shoulders and keeping his arms locked at the elbows.

As he lowers his stance and drops his hands to defend against the takedown, deliver a round kick to his head. Generally, pankratiasts favor punches and knees instead of kicks (high kicks in particular are used sparingly because they jeopardize balance), but for the more flexible combat athlete, they are effective in certain situations.

Step down with your right foot and land a right upper-cut to the jaw.

Returning to thesi machis, you sense that your foe is overly concerned with being taken down. Feint another shoot by making a sudden level change.

Clinch his neck and unleash knee strikes to the face.

SPRAWL COUNTER: CALF LOCK

Face off in opposite stances.

Shoot for a double-leg takedown.

Grip both of his lower shins and pull back on them, dropping your opponent face forward to the ground.

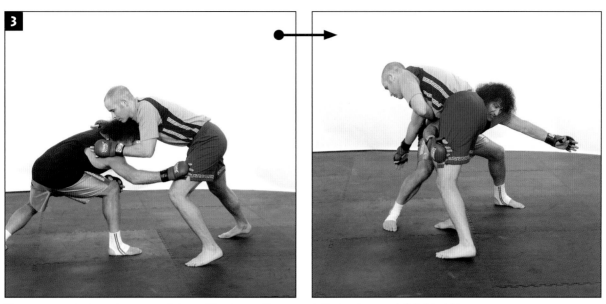

Your opponent attempts to sprawl to avoid going to the ground. Swing to your left behind him.

Follow up by slipping your right leg behind his left knee.

Grip your opponent's instep with both hands and push down on the foot, applying a crushing calf lock.

SUPLEX COUNTER: KNEEBAR

Face off in opposite stances.

Your opponent evades your jab, gets behind you and clinches you in a rear waist lock.

Step out to the right and bend forward to prevent the throw.

Continue your counter by grabbing his left ankle with both hands.

As your opponent begins to hoist you in the air for a suplex, wrap your left foot around his left leg and grip his wrists.

Fall back and to the right while holding your opponent's left leg. It is essential to keep the leg straight and wedged tightly against your body.

Use a tombstone grip (See close-up.), with your arms crossed around his ankle, and figure-4 your legs around his left leg. Thrust your hips forward to exert pressure on the knee and force your opponent to submit.

STANDING-CHOKE COUNTER: PUNCH TO HYPTIASMOS TO RASSEIN

You and your opponent face each other with opposite stances.

Taking the offensive, step in and feint a lead jab to the face.

Before he can sink his forearm into your throat, pin your chin against your upper chest while stepping in with your right foot deep between his legs. (This deep step is crucial.)

Sit back on the ground and push up on his thighs with both hands.

Change levels and shoot for a leg takedown. Before you can secure a good grip, your opponent catches you in a loose guillotine choke.

Use your right leg to assist in throwing him over your head.

DOUBLE-LEG TAKEDOWN COUNTER:
GUILLOTINE CHOKE TO HYPTIASMOS TO NECK CRANK

Your opponent shoots for your legs, and you respond by lowering your base.

He wraps both arms around your legs. Counter by wrapping your right arm around his neck for a guillotine choke.

Extend your legs and lift your opponent overhead.

Roll into a top-mounted position while maintaining your grip on his neck.

Fall back to the ground. Hook both legs inside your opponent's legs, behind the knees.

Shift your weight to the right, and crank your rival's neck in the same direction. It is essential to place your left knee on his stomach for added leverage.

ATTACKS FROM THE CLINCH

SHOULDER THROW TO ARMBAR

You and the opposing fighter are locked in a standing collar-and-elbow clinch.

Swim your right hand inside his left arm.

Straighten your legs and throw him over your right shoulder.

As your opponent lands, maintain control of his right arm and prevent a rollout by pushing down on his chest with your right hand.

While turning to the left, underhook your foe's left arm. At the same time, bend your knees and position your right hip under his hips.

With his right hand under your armpit, slip your left forearm behind his elbow. Slide your right knee onto his stomach and grab your right wrist with your left hand. Apply an armbar, arching back for added breaking pressure on the elbow.

CLINCH KNEE COUNTER:
TAKEDOWN TO ACHILLES LOCK TO KNEE WRENCH

From a tight neck clinch, your opponent pulls your head down to deliver a left knee strike. Keep your hands on his hips.

Remain as erect as possible and use both forearms to deflect the attack.

With your opponent on the ground, slide your arms back around his left ankle.

Arch back to exert pressure on his Achilles tendon until he taps. Place your left foot on his right leg to prevent an escape or a kicking counter from the ground.

As your opponent retracts his leg for another knee strike, quickly grip his left thigh with your right hand.

Grab his left leg with both hands and execute a high single-leg takedown.

If he fails to tap, pivot your left foot around the seized leg.

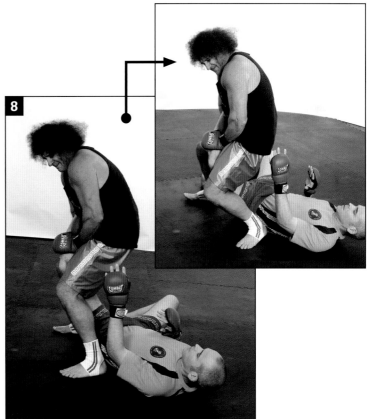

Sit back, exerting breaking force on the knee.

KEY LOCK AND TAKEDOWN TO SHOULDER LOCK

You and your opponent are locked in a loose clinch.

Move back slightly and slide your left hand down to grab your foe's right wrist. Loop your other hand over the top of his elbow.

Step forward with your left foot to the outside of his right foot.

Sit down while lifting your right leg between his legs. Torque your opponent's arm up at the same time.

Apply a key lock by grabbing your left wrist with your right hand.

Loop your left leg over his back and hook your right leg behind his right knee to prevent a forward roll (which would relieve pressure from the lock). Torque your opponent's arm up and back.

RASSEIN COUNTER: SCOOP THROW TO STRIKES

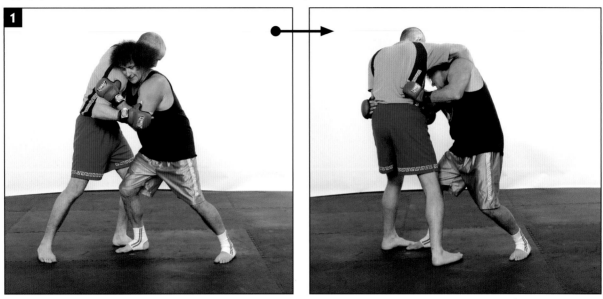

From a tight standing clinch, your opponent steps in with his right foot and swings his right arm around your neck in preparation for a hip throw. Instantly place your left hand on his lower back or hip to prevent him from pulling you over.

Throw him to his back.

Duck under his right arm.

Swing your left arm across his throat and scoop his right leg with your right hand.

Slide your right knee onto his chest and deliver an onslaught of punches to his face.

KEY-LOCK DEFENSE: TAKEDOWN TO CHOKE

You have your opponent in a rear waist lock. He attempts a key lock by grabbing your left wrist with his right hand.

Before your opponent can crank the arm counterclockwise, step quickly to your left and lock your hands. Wrap your left leg around your opponent's knee.

Bend your left arm to post on your elbow and roll to your left. Dig in the hooks.

Slip your left hand under his chin.

Trip him over your left leg and drive your chest forward, forcing him to the ground.

Now mounted on his back, release your hands and grab his right wrist with your right hand while posting on your left arm. Hook your right foot under his hip.

Lock in the rear choke by grabbing your right biceps with your left hand and driving your right hand behind his head. Push down with your head while squeezing your arms tightly together.

KATO (GROUND) TECHNIQUES
TOP-CONTROL ATTACKS

CHEST-PIN ATTACK: STRIKES TO SHOULDER CHOKE

From the chest mount, you prepare to deliver a straight punch to your opponent's face.

Your opponent wards off the blows with his forearms.

Your opponent attempts to stop your assault by pushing his right arm against your chest.

Slap the arm across his face with your left hand and lean forward.

Loop your shots around his blocks.

Slip your right arm under his head, grabbing the biceps of your left arm with your right hand. Place your left hand on his head.

Squeeze both arms together. Force added strangling pressure by pushing your head and upper body against his trapped right arm.

CHEST-PIN ATTACK: STRIKES TO ARMBAR

1

You are in top control and have your opponent tightly pinned, chest to chest. He prevents you from sitting up and striking by holding you in a neck clinch.

2

With your right hand, push your left forearm across his face. This move creates space and causes him to release his grip.

5

As you prepare another strike, trap his right arm with your left hand.

6

Quickly spin to your left, stepping over his head with your left foot. Grab his trapped right arm with both hands at the wrist.

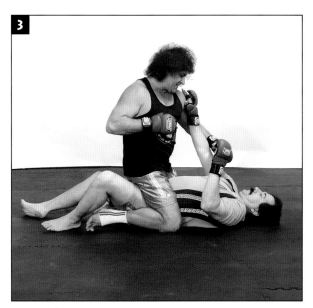

Sit straight up.

Deliver a downward punch to his face with your right hand.

Fall back while maintaining the grip on his arm.

With his elbow in your crotch area, elevate your hips and hyperextend the limb.

CHEST-PIN ATTACK: PUNCH TO KEY LOCK

You are top-mounted, chest to chest, with your left hand under your opponent's head.

You attack with right punches to his head, but he wards off the blows with his left arm.

Grab his left wrist with your left hand and push it to the ground. Slip your right hand under his left arm.

Slide your left arm under your opponent's neck and grab your left wrist with your right hand. Apply a key lock by lifting up on his elbow to torque his shoulder. It is essential to keep his hand on the ground and close to his body for maximum pressure.

Pull back your right arm as if to deliver another punch.

Post your right hand on the ground and push against his upper-left arm while crawling forward.

SIDE-PIN ATTACK: CROSS-SIDE ARMBAR

Your opponent is in side control, with his right arm trapped by your right arm.

Position your left leg across his face and fall backward, beside your opponent.

Posting on your left hand, step around his head while remaining close to his body.

Grab his right wrist with both hands and apply an armbar. Squeeze your knees together and raise your hips to apply pressure on the elbow.

SIDE-PIN ATTACK: KNEE STRIKE TO ROLLING LEG CHOKE

You have your opponent in side control, with your right hand flat on the floor on the far side of his body and your left hand under his head.

Raise your right leg and deliver a knee strike to the ribs.

Roll forward and to the right, causing your opponent to flip over.

Holding his left hand down with your right hand, swing your right leg over his body.

Tuck your right foot under his head and grip it with your left hand.

During the roll, let go of your foot and lock in a figure-four grip by looping your left leg over your right foot, tucking your instep behind your knee. If necessary, grab your right foot with your left hand to pull it into position. Pull his right arm across your body and tighten the lock.

You are now on the bottom, applying an inverted leg choke. With the choke securely locked, you can use your right hand to pull his head down, adding even more pressure.

NORTH-SOUTH PIN ATTACK

You are on top of your opponent in a north-south position, holding both his arms.

Release your right hand and dig a hook punch into his ribs.

Pivot to your right foot and trap his right arm near the elbow.

Sit down and post on your left hand.

3

As you recoil your right arm for another blow, he raises his right arm to block.

4

Step up on your left foot. Push down on his right arm with your left hand and slip your right hand below his right arm.

7

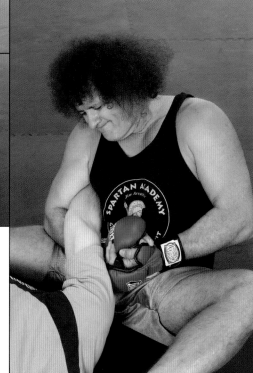

Lean back, applying an elbow lock. Place your left foot on his face to prevent him from escaping.

BOTTOM-POSITION TACTICS

CLOSED-SCISSOR ATTACK: SHOULDER LOCK TO STRIKES

Control your opponent's arms in a closed-scissor clinch from your back.

Turn off your left hip and slide to your right, bringing your right leg over your opponent's left shoulder. Grab his left arm with your right hand.

Cross your legs, post up on your left hand and lean forward.

Post on your left elbow and place your right hand on your opponent's back to prevent a rollout.

With your adversary defenseless and unable to move, cup your right hand under his chin and deliver finishing punches to the head.

OPEN-SCISSOR ATTACK: NECK-CRANK TURNOVER

1

With your opponent kneeling in your open scissors, post on your left hand and trap his head by looping your right arm around his neck.

3

Roll your opponent to your left, using your right leg to help sweep him over.

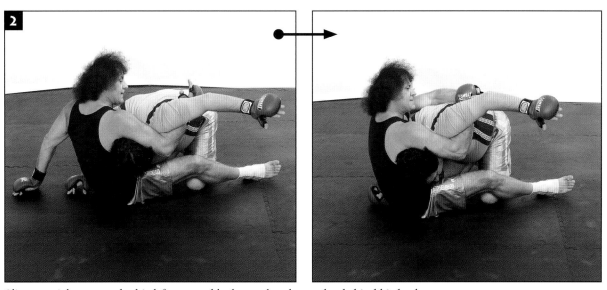

Slip your right arm under his left arm and lock your hands together behind his back.

Land in the mount and crank the head.

GROUND-AND-POUND COUNTER:
FOOT BLOCK TO PUSH-OFF TO KICKS TO REVERSE ARM LOCK

Your opponent is on his knees in your open waist scissors. He prevents you from sitting up by placing his right hand on your chest.

Immediately grab his right hand at the wrist. As he begins to deliver a punch to your face with his left hand, block it at the biceps with the heel of your right foot.

Loop your right knee over his right shoulder and raise your left foot.

Deliver a downward ax kick with your left heel to his back.

Push off his hip with your left foot and kick his head with your right heel. Maintain hold of his right wrist with both hands.

Slide back and pull your opponent down and forward by his right arm, yanking it out straight with the elbow facing up.

Loop your left leg over his lower back to prevent him from rolling to escape. Lift up on the wrist for optimal pressure and make him tap.

TOP-MOUNTED GROUND-AND-POUND COUNTER: KNEE BUMP TO HAMMER LOCK

Your opponent is mounted on your chest. Grip both of his wrists to prevent him from striking you.

Your opponent pins your chest with his left hand and disengages his right hand. As he prepares to strike you in the face with his right fist, grab his left wrist.

Continue to slide to the right and grip his left wrist behind his back with your left hand. Bend his arm at the elbow.

Raise your left hand to block the blow and slide your head to the right. Maintain the grip on his left wrist.

Use your left knee to strike him in the coccyx. This will bump him forward.

Using both hands, apply a hammer lock by pushing his left arm up and behind his back. Hook your legs behind his knees to prevent an escape by rolling forward.

SIDE-PIN ESCAPE TO REVERSE LEG CHOKE

You are on your back and your opponent has side control. His right arm is between your legs, and his left hand is under your neck.

Swing your leg around your opponent's head and pull his right wrist with your left hand. Block his left hip with your right hand.

Push off your left foot and lift your hips to the left. Drive your left forearm against his neck to create space.

Apply a figure-4 leg choke by looping your right leg over your left foot. Squeeze your legs together and pull on his right arm above the elbow with your left hand to submit him.

NORTH-SOUTH PIN TO BACK-MOUNT ESCAPE

You are on your hands and knees in a north-south position under the opposing fighter.

Your opponent quickly pivots to his left and mounts your back.

As he leans forward to apply a choke, use your right hand to block him from getting his arm under your chin.

Slip your right arm over his right elbow. At the same time, dip down and to the right.

Now on your back, your opponent punches your head. Defend by raising your right arm and post on your left hand.

Throw your foe off your back while maintaining a grip on his right arm.

Grab your left wrist with your right hand and push down against his elbow to submit him.

ARMBAR FROM NORTH-SOUTH POSITION

You have top control in the north-south position over your opponent, who is on his hands and knees.

Pull your right leg back.

Deliver a right knee strike to his face.

Turn your foe over to his back by lifting your right elbow and driving your weight to your left.

3

Wrap your right arm under his left armpit.

4

Lock your fingers together above his left shoulder. Bring both of your elbows in tight for greater leverage.

7

While maintaining hold of his left arm, drag your right foot next to his head, turn toward him and place your left knee on his left hip.

8

Fall back into the side armbar while sliding both hands to the wrist of the trapped arm.

NORTH-SOUTH POSITION BOTTOM-TO-TOP REVERSAL SUBMISSION

This is a counter to the previous sequence. This time, you are on the bottom and have your left arm locked.

Step out with your left foot and grip your foe's right arm above the elbow with your left hand. Post on your right hand.

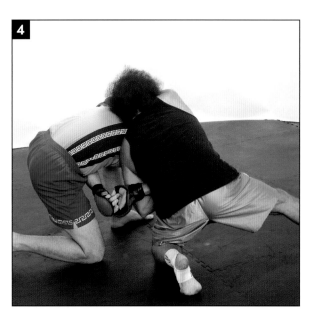

Turn to your right by pivoting on your left foot and shooting your right leg around your left.

Continue turning to the north-south position, and grab his right wrist with your left hand. Drop your chest on the back of his elbow, and apply a shoulder lock by lifting his arm with both hands.

3

Slide your head and right leg under his right armpit.

KLIMAKISMOS COUNTER: ARRICHION LOCK

From a seated position, your opponent has your back and attempts to apply a klimakismos. He has his hooks across your thighs. Sensing the choke, you raise your right arm to defend.

Use your left hand to bring his left foot over his right foot.

Still thwarting the choking attempt, lift your left leg over your opponent's top foot and lock your right knee over your left instep.

Arch back and raise your hips while pushing his right knee outward with both hands.

WAIST-SCISSOR COUNTERAS

STACK TO ACHILLES LOCK

You are standing inside your opponent's closed waist scissors. He intends to sweep you by grabbing your ankles. Clamp your knees together and bend forward while placing your hands on his chest.

Balance on your hands and move forward, turning your opponent onto his stomach.

Defend the sweep by falling forward rather than back. Post on your left hand.

Wrap your right arm around his left ankle and apply a figure-4 lock by gripping your left wrist with your right hand. Arch your torso back to exert pressure. Note that the right leg stays under his left calf; this creates a fulcrum to exert additional pressure.

SCISSOR ESCAPE TO HYPTIASMOS TO HEEL HOOK

As in the previous technique, you are standing in your opponent's open scissors and holding him down by pushing on his chest with both hands. He is holding both your ankles.

With your left hand, push your opponent's right knee outward and place your left knee inside his right knee.

Lock your hands together, cupping your right fist in the palm of your left hand. Twist to your left, torquing your opponent's heel. Make sure the instep is trapped in your armpit, with your wrist behind his ankle and your left forearm pushing down on the leg.

3

Fall back, wrapping his left ankle in the crook of your right elbow. At the same time, grab his right ankle with your left hand.

4

Loop your right leg over your opponent's left leg, locking it on his hip. Be sure to have your thigh behind his knee.

FOOT-LOCK COUNTER TO ELEVATOR SWEEP: ANKLE LOCK

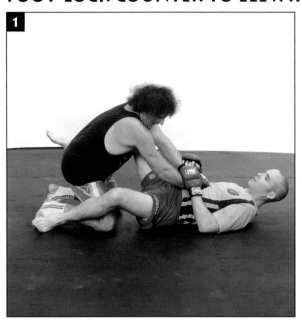

Your opponent has you in his open scissors and holds both of your wrists.

He sweeps you to the side by scissoring his legs, pushing with his right knee against the left side of your torso.

Pivot to your left until you are perpendicular to your foe. Wrap your left arm around his right ankle. Stop his forward movement by swinging your left leg over his trapped right leg and pushing your left foot into his chest.

3

Fall backward and drive your right knee between your opponent's legs to prevent him from mounting you.

5

Lean back and lock both hands together around the seized ankle. Arch your back and force your opponent to submit.

COUNTERS TO BLOCKED SUBMISSIONS (CHAINS)

BLOCKED ARMBAR TO LEG CHOKE

As you attempt an armbar, your opponent thwarts the attack by grabbing his right wrist with his left hand.

Post on your left hand and pull up on your opponent's arms with your right arm.

Fall back and bring your right leg over his neck. Grip your ankle with your left hand and loop your left leg over your right instep.

Loop your right leg inside his arms.

Remove your left leg, enticing him to sit up.

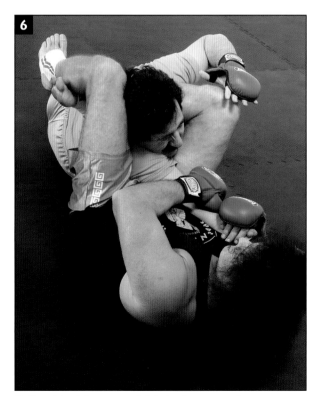

Pull on his right arm and tightly clamp your knees together, forcing his shoulder against the side of his neck.

Complete the leg choke by using both hands to pull down on his head.

STRIKES TO BLOCKED KEY LOCK TO ARMBAR

You are top-mounted and delivering punches to your opponent's face. He keeps his arms close to his head to shield himself from the assault.

Unable to get a clean shot, you attempt a key lock by pushing his left wrist to the ground with your left hand.

Pivot to the right and swing your left leg over his head. Use both hands to get a firm grip on his right arm.

Reacting to the submission attack, your opponent turns to his left and locks his hands together.

Fall back into an armbar, with the elbow locked in your crotch. Hold the arm tight against your chest so he cannot turn his arm to escape the hold. Keep your feet across his chest and neck, and elevate the hips.

BLOCKED CHOKE TO ARMBAR

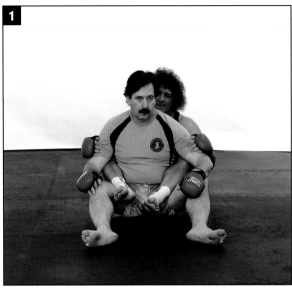

You have the opposing fighter's back in a sitting position.

Immediately, he senses a rear-choke attack and protects his neck by blocking with his left hand.

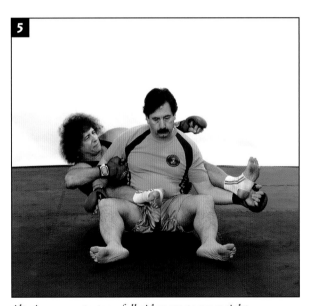

Altering your strategy, fall sideways to your right.

Sweep your left foot around to the far side of his face. Maintain the grip on his right arm with your right hand.

3

Use your left hand to pull his left arm down and away from the side of his neck.

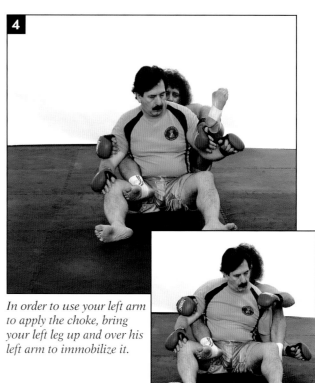

4

In order to use your left arm to apply the choke, bring your left leg up and over his left arm to immobilize it.

7

Grab his right wrist with both hands and use the strength of your left leg to force him back.

8

Fall back and execute an armbar.

15. FINAL THOUGHTS

Consider, if you will, the following dialogue from Plato's *The Myth of the Cave* (from the *Republic*):

SOCRATES: And now, let me give a parable to show how far our nature is enlightened or unenlightened. Imagine human beings living in an underground cave with an opening upward towards the light, which filters into the depths of the cave. These human beings have been here since birth, and their legs and necks have been chained so that they cannot move. They can only see what is directly in front of them, since they are prevented by the chains from turning their heads to either side. At a distance above and behind them is a raised path. And if you look closely, you will see a low wall built along the path, like the screen used by marionette players to conceal themselves from the audience while they show their puppets.

GLAUCON: I see.

SOCRATES: And if these prisoners were able to talk to each other, would they not suppose that the words they used referred only to the shadows that they saw on the wall in front of them?

GLAUCON: Of course.

SOCRATES: And if one of these prisoners were able at last to free himself, and explore to the upper world, would he understand what he saw?

GLAUCON: Not immediately.

SOCRATES: He would have to grow accustomed to the sights of the upper world. First he would be able to see the shadows best, next the reflections of men and other things in the water, and then the things themselves. Afterwards he would be able to gaze upon the light of the moon, the stars, and the spangled heaven. Would it not be easier at first for him to look upon the sky and the stars by night than upon the sun or the light of the sun by day?

GLAUCON: Certainly.

SOCRATES: And when he remembered his old habituation, and the wisdom of the cave and of his fellow prisoners, do you not suppose that he would be happy about his change and pity those who were still prisoners?

This story is symbolic of pankration's reincarnation in the late 1960s and the challenges it faced from the conventional martial arts establishment. Socrates described a man's liberation from darkness—a spiritual awakening to realism. Once he is freed from his physical restraints and leaves the cave, there is a rebirth of his senses. He comes to the understanding that the shadows envisioned in the cave were only reflections of what is real.

Just as there are no false shadows or imagery outside the cave, there are no preconceived notions of fighting in ancient Greece's ultimate sport. Unfortunately, these concepts were criticized and condemned three decades ago, when it re-entered mainstream martial arts. Many to this day continue to blindly accept unrealistic drills as the preferred means of learning to fight, although the numbers now competing in and practicing reality-based methods are on the rise.

To some, the idea behind mixed martial arts—combining techniques and skills from various sources—is novel. To present-day pankratiasts, however, this concept is nothing new, for their ancestors have been practicing this form of integrated combat for thousands of years. In this sense, the Hellenic martial way offers freedom to enable one to make his own conclusions. What the ancient Greeks have taught us is that no one style has a monopoly on the truth in combat. Each has its own special contributions to add to the pool of martial arts knowledge.

Art is a means of expression, which in turn is dependent on ideology. These ideas are born, flourish and decay, but they are not lost, nor do they perish; they persevere, and they sometimes move forward and evolve as a result of a new stimulus. The ideas behind modern pankration create efficiency in combat. They are not revolutionary but have been tested since early Western civilization. Similar to the Olympic ideal, pankration's goal is the comprehensive development of the mind, body and spirit through systematic participation in competition and training.

The Greek philosophers of antiquity indicated that combat sport transcended merely defeating one's foe in battle. Plato, Homer and others saw past the physical, brutal aspect of combat and provided detailed accounts of the areti that burned within the souls of the athletes in the heavy events. The boxers, wrestlers and pankratiasts were viewed as artists, like painters or sculptors, whose expression was found in the aesthetic of movement and in outthinking their opposition. Those who excel at modern pankration not only possess extraordinary athletic and technical prowess but also have the same dedication and self-knowledge cultivated by the ancient Greeks.

In conclusion, the Greeks were the first to develop and systematize a combat sport of integrated skills. It was also an attempt to promote martial competition at the Olympiad. Although it failed to endure the passing of time, its rebirth is indicative of the strength of its tradition, and its evolution coincides with and is symbolic of my own odyssey and that of every pankratiast: the endless journey of self-discovery.

APPENDIX I

TIMELINE OF PANKRATION'S EVOLUTION

The Bronze Age (1600 B.C. to 1062 B.C.)

- The first indications of athletic training and the competitive ideal appear in Minoan Crete. Games include tumbling, bull leaping, wrestling and boxing. These events take place during the festivals. (Their rules are unknown today.)

- Athletics develop rapidly in Mycenaean civilization. The general character of its society is more warlike than that of the Minoans.

- While some sports are copied from the Minoans, many are discarded, such as bull leaping and tumbling. Boxing and wrestling become the most popular sports during this time. Mycenaean colonists carry these to Cyprus.

- New, exciting contests are created, such as running and chariot racing, to enhance the competitive spirit. The most dangerous competition, *hoplomachia* (armed combat), is also developed.

- The Mycenaeans continue the tradition of holding athletic contests during religious festivals honoring the gods. At the same time, they establish funerary games to honor dead heroes.

The Geometric/Mythical Period (900 B.C. to 700 B.C.)

- The love of competition dominates Mycenaean life; young men pursue intense physical exercise, and leaders and heroes engage in and excel at competition.

- The funeral games held in honor of the slain Patroklos (described in the *Iliad*) include boxing, wrestling and armed combat.

- Athletes taking part in the games are not famous heroes but people from everyday life.

- Two important points emerge during this period: The people understand and value the necessity of diligent practice, and more important, society attaches high esteem to athletics and athletes. In the *Iliad*, army leaders, including Agamemnon himself, compete.

- The element of competition is equally vigorous throughout Greek mythology. Mortal men project their own passion to compete onto their gods and heroes.

- The *Gigantomachia*, the relentless battle between the gods and the giants, becomes symbolic of every conflict, especially between Greeks and barbarians.

- According to legend, Theseus and Herakles found *pankration*.

- Theseus passes pankration on to Athens, Arcadia, Miletus, Ephesus and the islands of Tenedos, Lesbos, Chios and Samos. Herakles passes pankration on to Sparta, Corinth, Peloponnesus, Italy and Sicily.

- *Pale* (wrestling) is entered into the Olympic Games in 708 B.C.

The Classical Period (700 B.C. to 342 B.C.)

- *Pyxmachia* (boxing) is entered into the Olympic Games in 688 B.C.

- Pankration is practiced in nearly all the Greek cities and colonies throughout the Mediterranean.

- Pankration is entered into the Olympic Games in 648 B.C. The rules prohibit biting and eye gouging.

- Sparta organizes its own local pankration festivals.

- In 564 B.C., the great Olympic champion Arrichion defeats his opponent with an ankle lock but is strangled to death in the process. The judges award the victory to his corpse.

- In 522 B.C., 10 master *pankratiasts* form a loose association to promote and preserve the concepts and techniques of their native combative art.

- In 480 B.C. at the Battle of Thermopylae, 300 Spartans, under the command of King Leonides, stop the advance of 10,000 Persian troops. Pankration skills are employed by the *hoplites*, who lose their weapons.

- In 406 B.C., Polydamos of Scottusa introduces pankration in Asia in the presence of the Persian Royal Court.

- Around 400 B.C., the pankratiast Damoxenus kills his opponent Creugas with a fingertip strike after fighting for hours without a decision.

The Hellenistic Period (342 B.C. to A.D. 18)

- In 336 B.C., the Athenian pankratiast Dioxippus accepts a challenge and soundly defeats Coragus, the best military warrior from Macedonia. Coragus carries body armor and a javelin, lance and sword, and Dioxippus competes naked, armed with only a club. The bout is attended by Alexander the Great. Later, Dioxippus is framed for theft and commits suicide.

- In 330 B.C., Alexander the Great introduces pankration to Persia.

- In 327 B.C., Alexander the Great introduces pankration to India.

- In 216 B.C., King Ptolemy IV of Egypt sends his best pankratiast, Aristonikos, to the Olympic Games with the goal of showing Egypt's superiority over Greece. However, the Theban pankratiast Kleitomachos prevails not by outfighting the Egyptian but by appealing to the patriotism of the Greek officials and crowd. The victory is a lesson on biased officiating, which existed even in ancient combat sport.

- Around 200 B.C., a boys' subdivision of pankration is added to the Olympic schedule. The inaugural winner is Phaidimos of Alexandria.

- In 180 B.C., master pankratiasts, seeing the decline of moral values in Greece, decide to discontinue teaching pankration publicly. Henceforth, only Olympic pankration was openly taught to the public.

The Imperial Period (146 B.C. to A.D. 18)

- In 146 B.C., mainland Greece succumbs to Rome in battle and Olympic pankration begins its decline over the next 100 years.

- The Romans institute new athletic festivals, many named after the Panhellenic games.

- The sport flourishes but differs from that of the Greeks. Rather than creating a religious connection or honoring dead heroes, emphasis is placed on providing brutal spectacles for the crowds.

- The Romans delight in the combat sports. *Capuan* boxing emerges, wherein contestants are armed with the weighted and spiked glove known as the *caestus*.

- Bloody contests between armed gladiators, or between men and wild beasts, become the favored spectacles for the mobs.

- Professional guilds, supported by the emperors, harm pankration and other sports. The great athletic tradition of Hellas is lost.

The Enlightenment Period (18 to 378)

- Pankration associations are found in Athens, Sparta, Crete, Alexandria, Antioch, Tarsus, Ephesus, Smyrna, Pergamos, Byzantium, Thessalonica and a few Aegean Islands.

The Byzantine Period (378 to 1458)

- With the power of Christianity in full force, pankration, along with all sports that worship Olympian gods, is eliminated from public life. The Olympics are held until 510, when Emperor Justinian abolishes them.

- Pankration's spiritual philosophy is codified into an advanced gnostic system, spanning a bridge between Christianity and paganism.

- Pankratiasts reveal some of their ancient texts and knowledge to the Byzantine imperial army.

- In Western Europe, Charlemagne sparks a cultural awakening by importing tutors to his court to teach Greek, Latin, astronomy, mathematics and pankration.

- A revival of pankration contests, called *clotsata*, is staged in Cyprus.

- In 1204, crusaders plunder the Byzantine Empire. As a result, mainland Greece and its islands are distributed among the crusaders, and many pankratiasts conceal themselves in the Greek mountains in order to preserve their knowledge and their art.

- In 1453, the remaining pankratiasts become freedom fighters in West Anatolia.

The Dark Ages (1458 to 1818)

- Occupied by the Turks, Greece falls into a dark age. Much knowledge is lost, and Greek science comes to a standstill. Small clans of pankration freedom fighters continue living in the mountains in mainland Greece and Western Anatolia. Slowly, they build a combat force and the resources needed to win their freedom from the Ottoman Empire.

The Renaissance Period (1818 to Present)

- Wealthy San Francisco sportsmen establish the Olympic Club, providing members the opportunity to stage reproductions of the games of ancient Greece and Rome. The most spectacular of these galas take place in 1895, when members of a local fencing club played the gladiators, and local boxers and wrestlers played the pankratiasts.

- With the revival of the Olympic Games, many attempts are made to return pankration to the competitions. However, all of them are unsuccessful. In 1895 the Cardinal of Lyon renders his official decision in this statement: *"Nous acceptons tout, sauf PANKRATION,"* meaning, "We accept all sports to be reinstated but PANKRATION."

- In 1898, efforts to reconstruct pankration for the modern age are documented in an article in *Health and Strength Magazine*. The author, R. Logan Browne, details his plans for the development of *neo-pancratium*.

- After World War I, Greece and Turkey continue to fight until 1922, when the Ottoman Empire dissolves into a republic.

- In 1923, pankratiasts from mainland Greece, Crete, Constantinople and Smyrna exchange techniques and re-establish their lineage.

- In the 1930s, pankration is revitalized when the few remaining clans merge their philosophies, principles and techniques.

- In the late 1960s, Jim Arvanitis introduces pankration to the mainstream martial arts community in the United States.

- In 1973, Jim Arvanitis is featured on the cover of *Black Belt* and in the first of hundreds of articles to follow. He starts a one-man mission to revive and popularize throughout the world the fighting art of his ancestors.

- In 1982, Jim Arvanitis creates the United Pankration Alliance, the objective of which is to represent the trained pankratiasts throughout the world.

- In the early 1990s, Greece attempts to resurrect pankration as their major self-defense system. Martial artists join with historians and military officials and get backing from the Greek government in this effort.

- Pankration begins to flourish throughout Europe and other parts of the world. Organizations form in France, Italy, Spain, Yugoslavia, Lithuania, Japan, Portugal and the Middle East.

- In 1998, the leaders of recently formed pankration organizations initiate dialogue to develop a standardized set of rules and protocol for international pankration competition. They also work to establish guidelines to present to the 2004 International Olympic Committee for acceptance.

- In December 2000, the IOC announces that pankration will not be part of the program in the 2004 Olympics.

- As the mixed-martial arts movement gains global popularity, pankration is recognized as the original mixed martial art and pankration events are held throughout the world.

APPENDIX II

CHRONOLOGY OF OLYMPIC COMBAT SPORT VICTORS IN ANTIQUITY

The following table lists the Olympic champions in wrestling, boxing and *pankration*, from the first known winner to the last. Gaps between contests indicate that there was no recorded victor or that the event was not held. Most of these names are taken from the men's division, although starting in 604 B.C. at the 44th games, youth division winners are also included.

Olympiad #	Year	Athlete	Event
18	708 B.C.	Eurybatos of Sparta	wrestling
23	688	Onomastos of Smyrna	boxing
27	672	Daippos of Kroton	boxing
32	652	Komaios of Megara	boxing
33	648	Lygdamis of Syracuse	pankration
36	636	Phrynon of Athens	pankration
39	624	Hipposthenes of Sparta	wrestling
40	620	Hipposthenes of Sparta	wrestling
41	616	Hipposthenes of Sparta	wrestling
42	612	Hipposthenes of Sparta	wrestling
43	608	Hipposthenes of Sparta	wrestling
44	604	Hetoimokles of Sparta	boys' wrestling
45	600	Hetoimokles of Sparta	wrestling
46	596	Hetoimokles of Sparta	wrestling
47	592	Hetoimokles of Sparta	wrestling
48	588	Pythagoras of Samos	boxing
52	572	Arrichion of Phigaleia Tisandros of Naxos	pankration boxing

Olympiad #	Year	Athlete	Event
53	568	Arrichion of Phigaleia Tisandros of Naxos	pankration boxing
54	564	Arrichion of Phigaleia Tisandros of Naxos	pankration boxing
55	560	Tisandros of Naxos	boxing
59	544	Praxidamas of Aigina	boxing
60	540	Milon of Kroton Leokreon of Keos	boys' wrestling boys' boxing
61	536	Rexibios of Opous	pankration
62	532	Eurymenes of Samos Milon of Kroton	pankration wrestling
63	528	Milon of Kroton	wrestling
64	524	Milon of Kroton	wrestling
65	520	Milon of Kroton Glaukos of Karystos	wrestling boxing
66	516	Timasitheos of Delphi Milon of Kroton	pankration wrestling
67	512	Timasitheos of Delphi Timastheos of Kroton	pankration wrestling
68	508	Kalliteles of Sparta	wrestling
70	500	Philon of Korkyra Agametor of Mantineia	boxing boys' boxing
71	496	Exainetos of Akragas Philon of Korkyra	wrestling boxing
72	492	Kleomeded of Astypalaia	boxing
73	488	Diognetos of Crete	boxing

Olympiad #	Year	Athlete	Event
74	484	Agias of Pharsalos Telemachos of Pharsalos Euthymos of Lokroi Epikradios of Mantineia	pankration wrestling boxing boys' boxing
75	480	Dromeus of Martineia Theagenes of Thasos	pankration boxing
76	476	Theagenes of Thasos Euthymos of Lokroi Theognetes of Aigina Agesidamos of Lokroi	pankration boxing boys' wrestling boys' boxing
77	472	Kallias of Athens Euthymos of Lokroi	pankration boxing
78	468	Epitimadas of Argos Epharmostos of Opous Menalkes of Opous	pankration wrestling boxing
79	464	Ephotion of Mainalos Diagoras of Rhodes Pherias of Aigina	pankration boxing boys' wrestling
80	460	Timodemos of Athens Amesinas of Barke Kyniskos of Mantineia	pankration wrestling boys' boxing
81	456	Timanthes of Kleonai Leontiskos of Messene Anthropos Phrynichos of Athens Alkainetos of Lepreon	pankration wrestling boxing boys' wrestling boys' boxing
82	452	Damagetos of Rhodes Leontiskos of Messene Kleodoros Apollodoros	pankration wrestling boys' wrestling boys' boxing

Olympiad #	Year	Athlete	Event
83	448	Damagetos of Rhodes Cheimon of Argos Akousilaos of Rhodes Polynikos of Thespiai Ariston	pankration wrestling boxing boys' wrestling boys' boxing
84	444	Taurosthenes of Aigina Alkainetos of Lepreon Charmides of Elis	wrestling boxing boys' boxing
85	440	Theopompos II of Heraia Gnathon of Dipaia	wrestling boys' boxing
86	436	Theopompos II of Heraia Pantarkes of Elis Philippos of Arkadia	wrestling boys' wrestling boys' boxing
87	432	Dorieus of Rhodes Lykinos of Elis	pankration boys' wrestling
88	428	Dorieus of Rhodes	pankration
89	424	Dorieus of Rhodes Kleomachos of Magnesia on the Maiandros Hellanikos of Lepreon	pankration boxing boys' boxing
90	420	Androthenes of Mainalos Amertas of Elis Theantos of Lepreon	pankration boys' wrestling boys' boxing
91	416	Androthenes of Mainalos Nikostratos of Heraia	pankration boys' wrestling
93	408	Polydamos of Scotussa	pankration
94	404	Promachos of Pellene Symmachos of Elis Eukles of Rhodes Peisirrhodos of Thourioi	pankration wrestling boxing boys' boxing

Olympiad #	Year	Athlete	Event
95	400	Antiochos of Lepreon Baukis of Troizen Demarchos of Parrhasia Euthymenes of Mainalos Xenodikos of Kos	pankration wrestling boxing boys' wrestling boys' boxing
96	396	Archedamos of Elis Bykelos of Sikyon	boys' wrestling boys' boxing
97	392	Euthymenes of Mainalos Phormion of Halikarnassos Neolaidas of Pheneon	wrestling boxing boys' boxing
98	388	Aristodemos of Elis Eupalos of Thessaly Antipatros of Miletos	wrestling boxing boys' boxing
99	384	Narykidas of Phigaleia Damoxinedas of Mainalos Alketos of Kleitor	wrestling boxing boys' boxing
100	380	Xenophon of Aigai Hippos of Elis	pankration boxing
101	376	Labax of Lepreon Kritodamos of Kleitor	boxing boys' boxing
102	372	Xenokles of Mainalos Thersilochos of Korkyra	boys' wrestling boys' boxing
103	368	Aristion of Epidauros	boxing
104	364	Sostratos of Sikyon	pankration
105	360	Sostratos of Sikyon Philammon of Athens Agenor of Thebes	pankration boxing boys' wrestling
106	356	Sostratos of Sikyon Chairon of Pellene Athenaios of Ephesos	pankration wrestling boys' boxing

Olympiad #	Year	Athlete	Event
107	352	Chairon of Pellene Athenaios of Ephesos	wrestling boys' boxing
108	348	Chairon of Pellene Aischylos of Thespiai	wrestling boys' wrestling
109	344	Chairon of Pellene Damaretos of Messene	wrestling boys' boxing
110	340	Asamon of Elis Telestas of Messene	boxing boys' boxing
111	336	Dioxippus of Athens Mys of Taras	pankration boxing
112	332	Cheilon of Patrai Satyros of Elis	wrestling boxing
113	328	Cheilon of Patrai Satyros of Elis	wrestling boxing
114	324	Astyanax of Miletus Douris of Samos	pankration boys' boxing
115	320	Astyanax of Miletus Hermesianax of Kolophon Pyttalos of Elis	pankration boys' wrestling boys' boxing
116	316	Astyanax of Miletus Choirilos of Elis	pankration boys' boxing
117	312	Aristophon of Athens	pankration
118	308	Antenor of Miletos Seleadis of Sparta Theotimos of Elis	pankration wrestling boys' boxing
119	304	Leontiskos Theotimos of Elis	pankration boys' boxing

Olympiad #	Year	Athlete	Event
120	300	Nikon of Anthedon Keras of Argos Archippos of Mytilene Hippomachos of Elis	pankration wrestling boxing boys' boxing
121	296	Nikon of Anthedon Amphiares of Sparta Kallippos of Rhodes Sosiades of Tralles Myrkeus	pankration wrestling boxing boys' wrestling boys' boxing
122	292	Philippos of Arkadia	boys' boxing
127	272	Nikarchos of Elis Kratinos of Aigeira	wrestling boys' wrestling
128	268	Alexinikos of Elis	boys' wrestling
131	256	Eikasios of Kolophon	boys' wrestling
133	248	Lastratidas of Elis	boys' wrestling
135	240	Kleoxenos of Alexandria Euanoridas of Elis	boxing boys' wrestling
140	220	Agesidamos of Messene	pankration
141	216	Kleitomachos of Thebes Paianios of Elis	pankration wrestling
142	212	Kapros of Elis Kleitomachos of Thebes	pankration and wrestling boxing
144	204	Damokrates of Tenedos	wrestling
145	200	Phaidimos of Alexandria Moschois of Kolophon	boys' pankration boys' boxing
147	192	Kleitostratos of Rhodes	wrestling
149	184	Epitherses of Erythrai	boxing
150	180	Epitherses of Erythrai	boxing

Olympiad #	Year	Athlete	Event
152	172	Diallos of Smyrna Agesistratos of Lindos	boys' pankration boys' wrestling
154	164	Lysippos of Elis	boys' wrestling
156	156	Aristomenes of Rhodes Amyntas of Eresos	pankration and wrestling boys' pankration
159	144	Xenothemis of Miletos	boxing
162	132	Menodoros of Athens	wrestling
172	92	Protophanes of Magnesia	pankration and wrestling
177	72	Sphodrias of Sikyon Isidoros of Alexandria Atyanas of Adramyttion Kalas of Elis Apollophanes of Kyparissia Soterichos of Elis	pankration wrestling boxing boys' pankration boys' wrestling boys' boxing
178	68	Stratonikos of Alexandria	pankration and wrestling
179	64	Stratonikos of Alexandria	pankration and wrestling
182	52	Marion of Alexandria	pankration and wrestling
185	40	Thaliarchos of Elis	boys' boxing
187	32	Thaliarchos of Elis	boxing
189	24	Glykkon of Pergamon	pankration
192	12	Polyktor of Elis	boys' wrestling
193	8	Nikophon of Miletos	boxing
194	4	Polyxenos of Zakynthos	boys' wrestling
198	A.D. 13	Aristeas of Stratonikeia	pankration and wrestling
201	25	Hermas of Antiocheia (Syria) Damokrates of Magnesia	pankration boxing

Olympiad #	Year	Athlete	Event
202	29	Hermas of Antiocheia (Syria) Damokrates of Magnesia	pankration boxing
203	33	Heras of Laodikeia (Phrygia) Damokrates of Magnesia	pankration boxing
204	37	Nikostratos of Aigai	pankration and wrestling
207	49	Tiberius Claudius Patrobius of Antiocheira Melankomas of Karia Publius Cornelius Ariston of Ephesos	wrestling boxing boys' pankration
208	53	Tiberius Claudius Patrobius of Antiocheira	wrestling
209	57	Tiberius Claudius Patrobius of Antiocheira	wrestling
211	65	Xenodamos of Antikyra	pankration
215	81	Tiberius Claudius Rufus of Smyrna	pankration
216	85	Titus Flavius Artemidoros of Adana	pankration
217	89	Titus Flavius Artemidoros of Adana Nikanor of Ephesos	pankration boys' pankration
218	93	Herakleides of Alexandria	boxing
219	97	Marcus of Antiocheia	boys' wrestling
220	101	Titus Flavius Archibios of Alexandria	pankration
221	105	Titus Flavius Archibios of Alexandria	pankration
224	117	Publius Aelius Aristomachus of Magnesia	boys' pankration
226	125	Deidas	boxing
227	129	Marcus Ulpius Domesticus of Ephesos	pankration

Olympiad #	Year	Athlete	Event
230	141	Marcus Tullius of Apameia (Bithynia)	boxing
231	145	Marcus Tullius of Apameia (Bithynia)	boxing
232	149	Sokrates Dionysios of Seleukeia	pankration wrestling
233	153	Marcus Aurelius Demetrios of Alexandria	pankration
236	165	Marcus Aurelius Chrysippos of Smyrna	wrestling
238	173	Marcus Aurelius Demosstratos Damas of Sardis Photon of Ephesos	pankration boxing
239	177	Marcus Aurelius Demosstratos Damas of Sardis Marcus Aurelius Hermagoras of Magnesia	pankration wrestling
240	181	Marcus Aurelius Asklepiades of Alexandria	pankration
243	193	Marcus Aurelius Asklepiades of Alexandria	wrestling
244	197	Marcus Aurelius Demos-Asklepiades of Alexandria	wrestling
246	205	Ploutarchos	boxing
247	209	Gaius Perelius Aurelius Alexandrus of Thyateira (Lydia) Gerenos of Naukratis	pankration pankration wrestling
248	213	Lucius Silicius Firmus Mandrogenes of Magnesia Aurelius Aelix of Phoenicia	pankration pankration wrestling

Olympiad #	Year	Athlete	Event
249	217	Aurelius Aelix of Phoenicia	pankration
250	221	Aurelius Phoibammon of Egypt	pankration
252	229	Apollonius	event unknown (wrestling, boxing or pankration)
253	233	Claudius Rufus (aka Apollonius)	event unknown (wrestling, boxing or pankration)

HEAVY EVENT OLYMPIC CHAMPIONS OF UNCERTAIN DATES

Ageles of Chios: boys' boxing

Brimias of Elis: boxing

Chaireas of Sikyon: boys' boxing

Dionysidoros of Mylasa: boys' boxing

Eualkidas of Elis: boys' boxing

Euanthes of Kyzikos: boxing

Nikosylos of Rhodes: wrestling

Pherenikos of Elis: boys' wrestling

Philles of Elis: boys' wrestling

Prokles of Andros: boys' wrestling

HEAVY EVENT OLYMPIC CHAMPIONS OF UNCERTAIN AUTHENTICITY

Marcus Aurelius Pappus of Myra: boxing

Aurelius Toalius of Oinoanda: pankration (twice)

Eudaimom of Egypt: boxing

Marcus Justius Marcianus Rufus of Sinope: boxing

Leukaros of Akarnania: pankration

Platon of Athens: wrestling

APPENDIX III

CATALOG OF PANKRATION SKILLS AND TRAINING

The following is an overview of the structural foundation of *pankration*, including modern *ano* (standing) and *kato* (ground) skills, and the techniques and training methods from the original combat sport, which form the nucleus of its restoration.

ANO (STAND-UP) SKILLS

- **Fundamentals**
  1. Readiness Position (*thesi machis*)
  2. Footwork/Mobility

- **Striking Tools**
  1. Precision Strikes (*daktylizein*)
  2. Punching (*pygmis*)
  3. Kicking (*laktisma*)
  4. Elbow Strikes (*agkohnizein*)
  5. Knee Strikes (*gonatizein*)
  6. Combinations

- **Clinch Fighting**
  1. Waist Locks (*mesolabe*)
  2. Neck Tie-Ups (*hamma*)
  3. Strikes From the Clinch
  4. Takedowns, Sweeps and Throws (*rassein apaly)*
  5. Standing Submissions (chokes and joint locks)

- **Defenses**
  1. For Strikes
     a. Blocks/Shields
     b. Parries and Scoops
     c. Evasions
  2. For Takedowns
     a. Redirection
     b. Jamming
     c. Sprawling
     d. Clinch and Strike

- **Other Ano Skills**
  1. Feinting
  2. Countering
  3. Defensive Hitting

KATO (GROUND) SKILLS

- **Top-Control Pins** (*epibasis*)
    1. Chest Pin (*pano thesi*)
    2. Back Pin (*thesi pano-plati*)
    3. Seated Ride Position
    4. Side/Cross Pin (*thesi katheta*)
    5. North-South Position
    6. Knee-on-Chest (*gonos sto stithos*)

- **Scissor Techniques** (*thesi psalidi*)
    1. Waist Scissors (open/closed)
    2. Single-Leg Scissors

- **Attack Methods**
    1. Striking
        a. From Top Control
        b. Ground Kicks
    2. Submission Holds
        a. Chokes
        b. Cranks
        c. Joint Locks
    3. Limb Destructions (Spartan pankration only)
    4. Throws and Sweeps

- **Additional Kato Skills**
    1. Bridging
    2. Posting
    3. Stacking
    4. Sit-Outs

- **Spartan Tactics**
    1. Biting (*dankonizein*)
    2. Gouging
    3. Finger Bending (*daktilolabe*)
    4. Hair Pulling

ANCIENT TECHNIQUES (PALAESMA)

The following techniques are the nucleus of the original Olympic sport pankration. They have been extracted from ancient resources, modified for optimum applicability, and codified in its modern derivative. This specific skill-set, referred to by Philostratos as *palaesma*, defines pankration's distinction among the vast array of martial arts in practice today.

• **Positions**
    1. *Thesi Machis* (ready position-stand-up)
    2. *Systasis* (frontal position-squared up to one's opponent)
    3. *Parathesis* (side position-i.e. side head lock, cross mount)
    4. *Epibasis* (mount-on chest and back)
    5. *Hyptiasmos* (on one's back-i.e., pulling guard)

• **Levels**
    1. *Ano Machia/Orthostandin* (stand-up fighting)
    2. *Kato Machia* (ground fighting)
    3. *Orthia Pale* (upright wrestling)
    4. *Kylisis* (ground wrestling without strikes)

• **Striking Techniques**
    1. Upper-Body Strikes
        a. *Enati Pygmis* (straight punch)
        b. *Evdomi Pygmis* (hook punch)
        c. *Triti Pygmis* (uppercut)
        d. *Mesi Pygmis* (body punching)
        e. *Ep Aroutrou* (hammer strike)
        f. *Vaseos* (palm strike)
        g. *Daktylizein* (finger strike)
        h. *Aghonizein* (elbow strike)
    2. Kicks (*Laktisma*)
        a. *Laktisma Eis Gastrizien* (straight kick with bottom of foot to stomach)
        b. *Laktisma Eis Gonoton* (straight kick with bottom of foot to knee)
        c. *Gonatizein* (straight knee kick)
        d. *Patima* (stomp kick)
        e. *Kato Laktisma* (up-kick from ground)

• **Locking/Submission Techniques**
    1. *Akrocheirismos* (finger bending)
    2. *Podolabe* (foot lock-heel hook, Achilles lock)
    3. *Trachelizein* (neck hold)
    4. *Akgonlabe* (armbar/elbow lock)
    5. *Gonatolavi* (kneebar)

- **Clinching (*Hamma*)**
  1. *Mesolabe* (waist lock)
  2. *Klimakismos* (grapevine body lock with legs)

- **Chokes/Strangulations (*Anchein*)**
  1. *Ano Piheio Anchein* (standing guillotine choke)
  2. *Kato Piheio Anchein* (guillotine choke on ground)
  3. *Anchen Meta Klimakismos* (rear choke with grapevine body lock)

- **Throws and Takedowns (*Rassein Apaly*)**
  1. *Embole* (single- and double-leg takedowns)
  2. *Saroma* (sweep)
  3. *Ankyrizein* (trip-leg hooking)
  4. *Tour de Hanches* (hip throw from head lock)
  5. *Ripsi Omoui* (shoulder throw with underhook)

- **Other Techniques**
  1. *Apekrousi* (defense)
     a. *Auchena periagein* (covering up one's face and sides of head from strikes)
  2. *Parakrouein* (feinting/distracting)

ANCIENT TRAINING METHODS (PARASKEVE)

- ***Palaistra/Gymnasia***

- **Trainers**
  1. *Gymnastes* (trainer of professional athletes)
  2. *Paidotribes* (polisher of the boy)

- **Basic Exercises**
  1. *Pneuma* (breathing)
  2. *Halterobolia* (weight training)
  3. *Pyx Atremizein* (strength development)
  4. *Skaperda* (rope pulling)
  5. *Anatrochasmos* (running backward)
  6. *Peritrochasmos* (running in a circle)

- **Combat Skills Development**
  1. *Cheironomia* (shadowboxing)
  2. *Skiamachia* (to fight with shadows)
  3. *Anapale/Pyrrhike* (mock fighting to music such as the lyre)
  4. *Akrocheirismos* (sparring drill allowing either light or full contact)

5. *Korykomachia* (to fight with bags)

6. *Schemata* (an instructional method of presenting the position of moves of pankration to the combat athlete)

7. *Palaeein* (special grappling drills whereby the pankratiasts were either covered with dust (*en te koeni*) or in mud (*en pilo*)

• **Equipment**

Spheres/Sphairai (safety gloves worn in training)

Amphotides/Epotides (special training headgear)

Strigil (a small, curved metal tool used by the athletes to scrape dirt and sweat from the body after a rigorous training session)

Korykos/Koryx (striking bags)

Besides the elements of ancient pankration, there were five contributors to the technical framework of modern pankration: Western boxing, *muay Thai*, Greco-Roman wrestling, freestyle wrestling and combat judo. The following were not part of original pankration but were added to the core skills. This integration produced a system that is more versatile and effective for present-day competition and personal defense.

• Elusive Footwork

• Defensive Parries and Evasions

• Shin Blocks and Elbow Strikes

• Precision Finger Strikes (*daktylizein*)

• Roundhouse Kick (*kildiki laktisma*)

• Side Kick (*plagion laktisma*)

• Neck Clinch and Knee Strike (*hamma kai gonatizein*)

• Cross Pin (*thesi katheta*)

• Kneebar (*gonatolabe*)

• Heel Hook

• Knee-on-Chest (*gono sto stithos*)

• Scissor Lock (fighting from one's back) (*thesi psalidi*)

• Greco-Roman Suplex Throw

• Go-Behind Ankle Pick

• Shoulder Choke (standing or on the ground)

• Strategic Setups and Countering

• Ground Grappling Escapes and Reversals

• Kinesiology/Body Dynamics for Maximum Hitting Power

• Leverage in all Grappling Applications

• Efficient Technique, as Opposed to Size and Strength

APPENDIX IV
MAP OF ANCIENT GREECE

Original map art created by Frank E. Smitha.

GLOSSARY OF BASIC TERMS

ACADEMIA (ah-cath-em-ee-yia): school for learning Hellenic combat arts.

AGKOHN (ah-gon): elbow

AGKOHNIZEIN (ah-gon-ee-zin): elbow strike

AGKOHNLABE (ah-gon-la-vee): elbow lock

AGONIS (ah-go-nees): contest

AGONISTIS (ah-go-nees-tee): competitor

AHAREEOS (ah-ha-ree-yos): learner, student

AIDOS (ah-ee-thos): honorable sportsmanship without arrogance

AKINITOPISI (ah-kee-nee-to-pee-see): immobilization

AKONITI (ah-ko-nee-tee): uncontested victory

ALINDESIS (ah-leen-thee-sees): rolling on ground

AMPHOTIDES (am-fo-tee-thees): helmets worn in sparring practice by ancient *pankrati-asts* to protect the head from injury

AMPROSTIO LAKTISMA (ahm-pros-tee-yo lak-tees-mah): front kick

ANHIN (ah-neen): strangulation

ANKYRIZEIN (ahn-kee-ree-zin): a trip or hook

ANO (ah-no) **PANKRATION**: upright fighting, similar to kickboxing, which specializes in striking techniques with fists, feet, elbows and knees, and also includes throws

APAGOREFSI (ah-pa-go-reph-see): tapout

APEKROUSI (ah-pee-kru-see): defense

APOFASI (ah-po-fa-see): decision

APOKLISMOS (ah-po-klees-mos): disqualification

APOPNIGMOS:(ah-pop-neeg-mos): stranglehold or choke

ARETI (ah-ree-tee): manly or martial virtue

ARHEGOS (ahr-he-yos): leader or master instructor

ATHLETIS (ah-thlee-tees): athlete

ATHLIMA (ah-thlee-ma): athletic/sport

AXINE (achs-zee-nee): battle ax

CAESTUS (ses-tus): Roman spiked and weighted gloves used in boxing and *pankration*

CHANCERY (chan-ser-ee): a popular ancient *pankration* technique involving the pulling of hair to gain leverage for one's blows

CHEIRONOMIA (hyea-ro-no-mee-yia): shadowboxing

CLOTSATA (clot-sa-ta): literally, "to cry out," a later form of Greek combat sport similar to *pankration*

DAKTILOLABE (thak-tee-lo-la-vee): finger lock

DAKTYLIZEIN (thak-tee-lee-zin): finger strike

DANKONIZEIN (than-ko-nee-zin): biting

DASKALOS (thas-ca-lo): teacher

DEETHAKTOR (thee-thak-tor): professor or senior trainer

DIALAMBANEIN (thee-ah-lam-ba-neen): waist hold

DOKIMOS (tho-kee-mos): beginner

DORY (tho-ree): spear

DRATTEIN (thra-teen): pulling

EFEDROS (eh-fee-thros): athlete who draws a bye in competition

EMBOLE (em-bo-lee): tackle

ENATI PYGMIS (ee-na-tee peeg-me): straight punch

EPIBASIS (eh-pee-ba-see): mount position

EPITHESI (ee-pee-thee-see): attack

EPIYLAKI (ee-pee-la-kee): on-guard

ENDYMA (en-thee-mah): training uniform

ERESTHE (eh-res-tee): team greeting

EP AROTROU (ahp ah-ro-tru): hammerfist

ERROSO (ee-ro-so): greeting to one person

ETIMI (eh-tee-mee): ready

EVDOMI PYGMIS (ev-tho-mee peeg-mees): hook punch

GANTIA (gan-tee-yia): fighting gloves

GASTRIZEIN (ga-stree-zin): stomach kick

GONOS EPANO TOU (go-no ee-pah-no too): knee top control

GONOS STO STITHOS (go-no sto stee-thos): knee on chest

GONI KADETON (go-nee ca-thee-ton): hook knee

GONATIZEIN (go-na-tee-zin): knee strike

GONATO (go-nah-toe): knee

GONATOLABE (go-nah-toe-la-vee): kneebar

GRODOS (gro-thos): striking with the open hand or closed fist

GYMNASION (gym-nah-see-on): gymnasium

GYMNASTES (gym-nas-tees): an athletic trainer who provided the special diet and exercises for the competitors in ancient Greece

HAMMA (ah-mah): clinch

HAMMA KAI GONATIZEIN (ah-mah kay go-na-tee-zin): clinch and knee

HELKEIN (cll-keen): pull

HELLANODIKES (el-len-oh-thee-kees): referee

HERETEESMOS (eh-ree-tees-mos): warrior salutation

HIMANTES (ee-mahn-tees): hand wraps of soft oxide worn by ancient Greek boxers

HITONA (ee-toe-na): uniform top

HOPLITES (op-lee-tees): foot soldiers in the ancient Greek military

HOPLOMACHIA (op-lo-ma-hee-yia): fighting with weapons

HOPLOMACHOS (op-lo-mah-os): weapons specialist/trainer

HOPLON (op-lon): the large round shield of a *hoplite*

HYPTIASMOS (eep-tee-yas-mos): back fall

HYSSOS (ee-sos): spear or javelin

ISOPALIA (ee-so-pah-lee-yia): draw

ISXIOU (ees-ix-ee-ou): hip throw

KARTEREIA (ka-te-ree-yia): toughness, endurance

KATO (kah-toe) **PANKRATION**: a rougher and more comprehensive form of the art that emphasizes ground combat and was preferred in the ancient Olympic Games (literally, "down *pankration*")

KATO PALE (kah-toe pa-lee): ground wrestling

KATO PYGMIS (kah-toe peeg-mees): ground and pound

KILDIKI LAKTISMA (keel-thee-kee lak-tees-mah): round kick

KIRIOS (kee-ree-yos): title for the grandmaster of the system

KLEOS (klee-yos): immortal glory

KLIMAKISMOS (kleem-ah-kees-mos): a grappling maneuver in which a fighter jumps on his opponent's back and applies a choke while scissoring his abdomen ("ladder trick")

KLIMAX (klee-max): an agreement between two fighters to trade unblocked blows until one fighter collapses, making the other the victor

KOPIDIAN (ko-pee-thee-on): a slashing knife or dagger

KOPIS (kop-ees): a slashing sword used by Greek *hoplites* in warfare

KORYKEOIN (ko-ree-kee-yon): a special room in the *palaistra* equipped with training apparatus for boxers and *pankratiasts*

KORYKOS (ko-ree-kos): suspended heavy bags

KORYKOMACHIA (ko-ree-ko-ma-hee-yia): bag training

KORYX (ko-reex): see *korykos*

KRANOS (kra-nos): headgear

KREITAS (kree-yee-tees): judge

KYLISIS (kee-lee-sees): wrestling on the ground

LAKTISMA (lak-tees-mah): kicking or striking with the foot

LONCHE (lon-chee): spear or javelin

MACHAIRA (mah-heh-ree): a large knife or a curved sword or sabre (see *kopis*)

MACHITIS (mah-hee-tees): fighter

MAHITIKI TEHNI (ma-he-tee-kee ten-ee): the native Greek term meaning "martial art"

MASELA (mah-see-la): mouthpiece

MESI PYGMIS (meh-see peeg-mees): body punching

MESOLABE (meh-so-la-vee): waist lock

MESI LAKTISMA (me-see lak-tees-mah): kick to the body

MU TAU (mee-teff): the Greek-letter acronym for *mahitiki tehni* (martial art)

MU TAU PANKRATION: synonym for *panmachia*

MYRMEX (meer-mex): a lethal form of *himantes* designed to enhance a Greek boxer's striking effectiveness in competition

NIKITIS (nee-kee-tees): winner of a contest

ORTHIA PALE (or-thee-yia pah-lee): upright wrestling that includes clinching, takedowns and throwing techniques

ORTHOSTADIN (or-tho-stah-deen): standing combat

OTHISIS (oh-thee-sees): thrust kick

PAIDOTRIBES (pa-ee-tho-tree-vees): in ancient Greece, a trainer of unarmed combat skills

PALAISTRA (pah-lay-stra): ring area (modern) or training hall (classic)

PALE (pah-lee): wrestling

PAMMACHON (pah-mah-kon): the integrated combat art used before sport *pankration* (literally, "total fight")

PANKRATIAST (pan-crat-tee-ist): one who practices or competes in *pankration*

PANKRATION (pa-gra-tee-on/pan-cray-shun): an ancient Greek combat sport introduced in the Olympic Games in 648 B.C. Intended to simulate unarmed combat training for war, it featured both standing and ground skills, had a limited number of rules and embraced submission techniques as a means of defeating one's adversary (literally, "all powers")

PANMACHIA (pahn-mah-hee-yia): a system of unarmed battlefield combat with no restrictions on the concepts and methods used (see *pammachon*); dates back to the earliest times of recorded Hellenic history (literally, "total fight")

PANO THESI (pa-no thee-see): top-control position or chest mount

PAPHSATE (paf-sa-tee): a referee's call to stop fighting

PARADINESE (pah-ra-thee-nees): "Do you give up?"

PARADINOME (pah-ra-thee-no-me): "I surrender"

PARATHESIS (pa-ra-thee-sees): sideways stance

PARAZONE (pah-ra-zo-nee): a dagger used in extremely close-quarters battlefield combat (literally, "side belt")

PATIMA (pah-tee-ma): stomp

PERIODONIKES (peh-ree-oh-thon-ee-kees): special title given to the victor of the four major ancient festivals: Olympia, Delphi, Corinth and Nemea

PIHEIO AHNIN (pee-he-yo ah-neen): rear stranglehold using the forearm

PLAGION LAKTISMA (pla-gi-yon lak-tees-mah): side kick

PNEUMA (new-mah): breathing exercises similar to those used in yoga or meditation (literally, "breath," "air" or "spirit")

PODI (po-thee): foot

PODIZEIN (po-thee-zin): foot strike

PODOLABE (po-tho-la-vee): foot lock

POLEMIKOS (po-lee-mee-kos): combat athlete

PROPONITIS (pro-po-nee-tees): coach

PYGMIS (peeg-mees): boxing (fist and open-hand strikes)

PYRRICHIOS (pee-ree-kee-yo): in ancient Greece, a war dance practiced with weaponry that resembled choreographed fighting

PYX (peex): fistfighting, boxing

RASSEIN (rah-seen): throw to ground

RAVDOS (rahv-thos): referee's stick

ROPOLO (rho-po-lo): a club (the primary weapon of Herakles)

SAGARIS (sa-ga-rees): battle ax

SARISSA (sa-ree-sa): a heavy Macedonian thrusting spear

SAROMA (sa-ro-mah): sweep

SAUNION (saw-nee-on): a javelin thrown at one's opponent from long distances

SCHOLEIO (skoo-lee-yoo): school

SINTAXIS (seen-tax-ees): "attention" or "line up"

SIRA (see-ra): weight divison

SKIAMACHIA (skee-yia-ma-he-yia): shadow fighting with weapons

SKINAKI (skee-na-kee): jump-rope

SPADE (spa-thee): broad, double-edged sword

SPHAIRAI (sfay-ray): padded gloves

STADAIA PALE (sta-thay-ya pa-lee): upright grappling

STAMATA (stah-ma-ta): referee's call, meaning "stop"

SYSTASIS (see-stah-thees): square, upright stance

TAXIS (taachs-ees): grade level

THESI KATHETA (thee-see kah-thee-tah): cross-mount or perpendicular position

THESI MACHIS (thee-see mah-hees): fighting stance

THESI PANO-PLATI (thee-see pah-no pla-tee): rear-mount position

THESI PSALIDI (thee-see sa-lee-thee): scissor position

THRATOME (thra-toe-may): grappling

TRITI PYGMIS (tree-tee peeg-mees): uppercut

TRACHELIZEIN (tra-keh-lee-zin): neck hold

VOETHOS (vo-yee-thos): assistant instructor

XIPHOS (zee-fos): a straight-bladed, doubled-edged sword used for slashing and thrusting

XYELE (zee-lee): curved dagger or sickle

YEOSKELIZEIN (yo-skee-lee-zin): foot sweep

BIBLIOGRAPHY

Arvanitis, Jim. *Mu Tau: The Modern Greek "Karate."* New York: Todd & Honeywell, 1979.

Arvanitis, Jim. *Pankration: The Traditional Greek Combat Sport and Modern Mixed Martial Art*. Boulder, CO: Paladin Press, 2003.

Butler, Samuel (translator). *Homer: The Iliad and the Odyssey*. New York: Barnes and Noble Books, 1999.

Cartledge, Paul. *The Spartans: The World of the Warrior - Heroes of Ancient Greece, From Utopia to Crisis and Collapse*. New York: Vintage Books, 2003.

Gardiner, E. N. *Athletics of the Ancient World*. London: Oxford University Press, 1930.

Gardiner, E. N. *Greek Athletic Sports and Festivals*. London: MacMillan and Company, 1910.

Gardiner, E. N. *Olympia: Its History and Remains*. London: Oxford University Press, 1925.

Gardiner, E. N. *The Pankration and Wrestling. Journal of Hellenic Studies*, 1906.

Golden, Mark. *Sport and Society in Ancient Greece*. New York: Cambridge University Press, 1998.

Hale, William Harlan. *Ancient Greece*. New York: iBooks Inc., 2001.

Harris, H. A. *Greek Athletes and Athletics*. London: Cornell University Press, 1966.

Harris, H. A. *Sport in Greece and Rome*. London: Cornell University Press, 1972.

Kyle, Donald. *Athletics in Ancient Athens*. Leiden, Netherlands: Brill Academic Publishers Inc., 1987.

Logan-Browne, R. *Neo-Pancratium. Strength and Health Magazine*, London: 1898.

Mannix, Daniel P. *Those About to Die: The Way of the Gladiator*. New York: iBooks Inc., 2001.

Mavromataki, Maria. *Greek Mythology and Religion*. Athens, Greece: Haitali, 1997.

Miller, Stephen G. *Areti: Greek Sports From Ancient Sources*. London: University of California Press Ltd., 1991.

Olivova, Vera. *Sports and Games in the Ancient World*. London: St. Martin's Press, 1984.

Pangle, Thomas L. (translator). *The Laws of Plato*. Chicago: University of Chicago Press, 1988.

Pressfield, Steven. *Gates of Fire*. New York: Bantam Books, 1998.

Scanlon, Thomas. *Greek and Roman Athletics: A Bibliography*. Chicago: Ares Publishers Inc., 1984.

Warry, John. *Warfare in the Classical World*. London: Oklahoma Press, 1995.